The Positive Psychology Workbook Series

Invitation to Positive Psychology:
Research and Tools for the Professional
Robert Biswas-Diener

Positive Identities:
Narrative Practices and Positive Psychology
Margarita Tarragona

Positive Motivation
Kennon Sheldon

Positively Happy:
Routes to Sustainable Happiness
Sonja Lyubomirsky & Jaime Kurtz

Positively Mindful:
Skills, Concepts, and Research
Donald Altman, M.A., LPC

Positive Acorn

http://www.positiveacorn.com

Table of Contents

Week One: What, and why, is positive psychology?

Welcome to this course on positive psychology. You may have joined the course for any number of reasons…. Perhaps you are looking for new tools that will give you an edge at work, or think that a focus on the positive aspects of human psychology is a refreshing counterpoint to looking at depression or other problems. Maybe the course was recommended by a friend, or possibly you read a popular book on happiness that piqued your interest or helped you in your own life. Whatever the reason, I am pleased to announce that positive psychology has a little something for everyone. It is not a self-help movement or a re-packaging of "the power of positive thinking." It is not American-style "happy-ology," and it is not a passing fad. Nor does understanding this exciting new discipline require a doctorate in psychology.

Positive psychology is the scientific study of human flourishing, and an applied approach to optimal functioning. The lessons and applications of positive psychology research are appropriate to everyone, and I mean literally everyone. The research that forms the foundation of positive psychology has been drawn from teenagers and the elderly, executives and tribal people. The measures and practical applications that make up the toolbox of positive psychology can be applied across all domains of life. Chances are, you came to this course hoping to gain knowledge and skills you can use in your professional life, whether you are an educator, therapist, coach, manager, human resource worker, or medical programme evaluator. If so, positive psychology in general, and this course in particular, definitely has something to offer you. Importantly, however, the major lessons and important points contained in this course can be as applicable to you personally—in your own life at home—as they are to you professionally. In the last decade or so, positive psychology research has produced many new insights—many of them counter-intuitive— into when and how people function best. In this course, you will be introduced to the foundational studies of positive psychology, as well as to the newest theories and latest interventions

At its heart, positive psychology is a radical idea. If you are anything like me, you probably spend at least a portion of each day worrying about what could go wrong, complaining about what did go wrong, beating yourself up for opportunities missed, or feeling frustrated with life's many set-backs and disappointments. This makes sense…. There is much to worry about and complain about: housing prices are high, commutes are tiresome, organisational culture can be frustrating, and our clients, employees, colleagues, and supervisors can be a challenge. In fact, there is a body of research evidence that shows that folks are actually "hard-wired" to pay attention to threats and problems.[1] From an evolutionary point of view, being vigilant for all that could go wrong makes sense. Problems often require an immediate response, and—at least historically speaking—the people who were better able to adapt quickly and respond to threats were better able to survive and function. Being alert could have helped certain people distinguish between sticks and snakes on the ground or given precious time to escape when seeing a predator approach.

From the long perspective of evolutionary history, this all makes logical sense. But, what might seem logical in the case of poisonous snakes or sabre toothed tigers likely does not hold true for your current career. Missed deadlines, communication difficulties, and problems with productivity are not matters of life and death, even though they feel pressing. The same vigilance that might be so important to pre-industrial tribal people living in inhospitable places may not translate well to the average urban commuter or office worker. It makes sense, then, to take a step back and ask yourself: How is my vigilance for problems helping me? And—perhaps more importantly—is paying attention to what does and could go wrong the best route to accomplishing my goals?

1.1 Reflection

Take a moment to reflect upon and answer these important questions:

What types of problems am I often on the lookout for? At home? At work?

What are the benefits of keeping a keen eye out for things that might go wrong? How might this tendency affect my ability to prepare for, or respond to, problems?

What are the costs of a problem focus? What might I be missing while my attention is otherwise trained on potential problems?

To this last question positive psychology provides a revolutionary answer: try looking at the positives, and what could go right, and see what this new approach buys you. Instead of planning for and dealing with problems, positive psychology suggests that it might be fruitful to look at opportunities, successes, and strengths, as we go about the business of living. Please do not make the mistake of thinking that I—or any other positive psychologist—advocates only a positive perspective approach to life. Indeed not. I see tremendous wisdom in accurately predicting problems and being aware enough to see troubles in their early stages. Too often, however, downside risk, setbacks, and pitfalls take up the lion's share of our attention. Positive psychology merely makes the suggestion that there is much to be gained in expanding your focus to include life's better points. This is more than a philosophical approach of looking at the world through rose-tinted glasses; there is strong empirical support that a solutions orientation and strengths focus actually work, as we will discuss in detail below.

What is Positive Psychology?

In many ways positive psychology is not a new concept. Students of philosophy will recognise that great thinkers throughout the ages have attended to matters of the good life and living a moral and virtuous existence. In ancient Greece, for instance, Aristotle wrote the *Nicomachean Ethics*, in which he outlined the good life for the individual and the community. He suggested that happiness included materially favourable circumstances, pleasant feelings, and living in accord with one's virtue. Aristotle also emphasised civic responsibility as an integral part of individual success. Other philosophers from the classical Greek period emphasised personal freedom, the pursuit of pleasure, and the development of self-control as crucial components to the good life.

Religious texts and spiritual leaders throughout history have likewise emphasised the importance of good living and positive character. Even a cursory look at the Western monotheistic religions, for example, suggests that certain personal virtues such as forgiveness, self-sacrifice, faith, and loyalty are commonly prescribed as being among the most valuable attributes, and those that are likely to lead to success in this world and—according to scripture—reward in the next. In recent times thought leaders of the humanistic movement have emphasised the possibility of individual growth. Humanistic theorists such as Abraham Maslow discussed basic human needs such as food, shelter, and relationships as antecedents to the larger human endeavour of self-determination and self-actualisation.[2] In each case—philosophy, religion, and humanistic psychology—

there was a basic assumption that people are capable of "goodness" and that they can "become better." These intellectual and spiritual forebears paved the way for the modern advent of positive psychology. What distinguishes positive psychology from these other approaches—or from self-help books for that matter— is an emphasis on careful empirical research. Instead of relying on reasoning, intuition, or folk wisdom, empirical researchers look to the observable world for testable theories and provable explanations. Positive psychology represents, in many ways, a shift from faith to evidence.

Positive psychology is not a *philosophy* of the world. Positive psychology is a *science*, and brings the many virtues of science—replication, controlled causal studies, peer review, representative sampling (to name a few)—to bear on the question of how and when people flourish. In the late 1990s psychologist Martin Seligman, then president of the American Psychological Association, noticed that the vast majority of psychology was problem focused. In the years immediately following World War II there was an intense amount of attention given to the pressing problems of trauma and depression, and this period was instrumental in defining the focal legacy of modern psychology. Most research and intervention over the last half century has aimed at addressing the important problems of anxiety, depression, schizophrenia, suicide, and drug abuse. This psychology, according to Seligman, was really only half a psychology and was more focused on mental illness than mental health. Seligman is incredibly well read and he was familiar with the philosophical and religious traditions which asked important questions about virtue, the good life, moral behaviour, and other positive aspects of living. Influenced by these traditions, Seligman suggested, as part of his official presidential platform, that we begin asking "what is going *right* with people" as well as what is wrong with people. He used his professional position to establish a new branch of science called positive psychology.

In its early days, positive psychology was cobbled together from a handful of maverick yet productive researchers who happened to be working on unusual questions about positive topics. These were scientists who were studying hope, happiness, play, creativity, wisdom, and gratitude, among other things. Seligman used his considerable influence to bring together these pioneers and establish a loosely organised body of research literature that spoke about people at their best. Of course, just as Seligman was not the first person in history to attend to thriving, nor was he the first to coin the phrase "positive psychology." This term appeared in print, used by Maslow, as early as 1954, and may even pre-date that time. In fact, because modern positive psychology, in its nascent days, was based heavily on a social network in social, personality, and clinical psychology, some important players were not "invited to join the game," as it were.

These included researchers in humanistic psychology, philosophers, coaches, sports psychologists, developmental psychologists, and others—many of whom have since made important contributions to the evolution and growth of positive psychology. But, in those early days, Seligman and his pioneering positive psychology colleagues hoped to earn a place at the table of the historical discussion of the good life by contributing brand-new insights based on a specifically *scientific* understanding of many of these concepts. And it worked. For a variety of reasons—its empirical foundation, its positive emphasis, Seligman's effortful popularisation, the psychological climate in the wake of the September 11th terror attacks—positive psychology caught on. The movement provided a home for scholars hoping to research meaning in life, character strengths, and other topics related to optimal functioning. Similarly, businesses were attracted to the model because it had the potential to provide valuable insights into motivation, productivity, and high performance. Educators saw the value in using student assets to improve learning. Counsellors recognised the utility of tapping strengths to overcome problems. Even the general public took to the topic. For lay people, positive psychology offered a re-defined approach to self-help and self-growth based on cutting edge science. Although some of the messages coming out of the movement were common sense, or reiterations of older self-help advice, the foundation of science upon which positive psychology is built offered the promise of a trusted method to tell the good advice from the bad, the effective tools from the fads.

Today, positive psychology has evolved from a hodgepodge group of academics studying a relatively narrow range of topics in the United States to a burgeoning movement of professionals from all around the globe. This is an important point because it is easy to imagine a scenario in which this field could have remained distinctly American. It will come as a great relief to those who are concerned about the cultural appropriateness of positive psychology to learn that there are experts with productive research agendas in societies as diverse as England, Israel, the Netherlands, India, Hong Kong, Singapore, and Korea, to name only a few. A very real testament to the broad international appeal of positive psychology can be seen in even the single example of the *1st Applied Positive Psychology Conference* that CAPP organised at the University of Warwick (UK), in April 2007. This meeting alone was attended by 230 delegates from 24 different countries, including Australia, Brazil, Iceland, and Japan. There is even a new—as of this writing—International Positive Psychology Association (see **www.ippanetwork.org**), which seeks to facilitate increased global collaboration and cooperation. Positive psychology has also become more sophisticated in its methods, more applied, and has a more cohesive identity than in its early days. Positive psychology is now commonly defined as "The scientific study of optimal functioning." Occasionally, you come across a definition such as "positive psychology is the scientific study of strengths, optimism, and happiness," or "positive psychology is the scientific study of what goes right in life." As you can clearly see, these are all variations on a theme. In each case the emphases are on the scientific underpinnings of field and the positive, non-clinical focus of these studies. Thought leaders in the field such as University of Michigan psychologist Chris Peterson describe positive psychology as having three major foci. These include a focus on positive subjective states such as happiness, positive traits such as character strengths, and positive institutions such as schools or businesses. These broad categories define, although not officially perhaps, the bulk of the research and application of positive psychology.

One of the most interesting trends in the evolution of positive psychology is its transformation from a basic science to an increasingly applied science. If, in its infancy, positive psychology was about charting the waters so to speak; that is, establishing research programmes on strengths, optimism, and happiness…. It is now about how best to use the results of these studies to develop strengths, increase optimism and happiness, and promote optimal functioning. In short, it has moved from a fairly *descriptive* discipline to a more *prescriptive* discipline. We now know enough about topics like positive emotion and character strengths to be able to create effective interventions and apply our learning to a variety of domains ranging from workplace culture to team building to therapy to designing more effective educational curricula.

The good news is that positive psychology works! A large body of research evidence is showing the promise of a strengths-based focus and the power of positive emotion: students appear to gain more by working with their strengths than focusing their energies on shoring up weaknesses;[2] therapies with a solutions focus are known to be more brief than long-lasting counselling techniques such as psychoanalysis;[3] businesses seem to profit by attending to workers' best qualities and capitalizing on these.[4] Positive psychology transcends simple self-help advice or common sense wisdom by adding a much needed empirical burden of proof to its claims. As Jim Clifton, the CEO of the Gallup Organization once said, "I use positive psychology in my organisation because the research shows it works. If the research showed that yelling at my employees worked better, I would do that instead." Whether he meant his words to be taken literally or not, his comments illustrate that positive psychology has been noticed by leaders in the business world – as CAPP's work with leading international organisations such as Unilever and Norwich Union shows – as they have by coaches, therapists, and educators. Positive psychology works, and in this course you will learn how to make it work for you.

Why a Positive Focus?

It probably goes without saying that there are many people who are sceptical of the positive psychology approach. For most folks, it just makes sense to pay attention to under-performing workers or to try to tackle client problems. And what of all those things that are going well? The implicit message seems to be, "Why rock the boat?" Why waste time honing strengths when you could be undertaking the important work of shoring up weaknesses? An interaction I had recently with a student of mine at the Portland State University sums up this point of view nicely: I assigned the students an activity in which they were to choose one of their top strengths and let it act as a guiding theme for one week. That is, every time they came upon a difficulty, had to make an important decision, or needed to perform well they were to think of their strength and ask "How can using this strength help me in this situation?" At the end of the week the students turned in a short paper discussing the outcome of this strengths-based experiment. The very first paper I picked up said the following:

"This week I decided to choose one of my weaknesses and tried to work on it. I know the assignment was to choose a strength but I figured since my strengths come naturally to me anyway there is not really any point in working on them."

The paper went on to describe his struggles with tardiness and I went on to give him very little credit for the assignment. My student missed a very fundamental point: It turns out, and this may be counter-intuitive to some people, that using strengths and tapping positivity can provide larger gains than dealing with weaknesses and focusing on problems. And there is exciting proof for this position.

One area that has received the largest amounts of attention from positive psychology researchers is business and organisations. Positive psychology studies have shown tremendous benefits of positivity in the workplace. The Gallup Organization reports that "disengaged workers" cost companies billions of dollars a year in lost customers, healthcare, and turnover cost.[5] Happy workers, by contrast, are more likely to receive high supervisor and customer evaluations, take fewer sick days, show up to work on time, help their colleagues, make more money, and solve problems creatively.[6] Happiness doesn't just feel good, it is good for you (and your clients and your office). Gallup studies also show that top managers spend quality time with their most productive workers and explicitly try to match strengths to projects; and that workers are more productive when they have the opportunity to "do what I do best each and every day."[7]

Assignment for clients/ workshops

Of course, the workplace is not the only place where positive psychology is useful. Educators have turned a keen eye toward examining student strengths, and how school can be optimally designed to promote learning. Programmes have been geared toward teaching young people everything from character to leadership, resilience to gratitude. There is a growing understanding that students respond well to positive expectations, and that having the opportunity to employ their strengths can boost their self-esteem. In one study undertaken in the American Midwest, students of all reading abilities were taught a speed reading method. While a traditional weakness-focus approach would suggest that poor readers have much to gain from special educational programmes, it was the top readers who advanced the most—increasing from an average of 300 words a minute to 2,900 words![8] Increasingly, top private schools in Australia and North America are incorporating positive psychology into every aspect of their curricula, to give their students a competitive edge. At CAPP, our colleague Jenny Fox Eades is working in partnership with UK schools to enhance the natural strengths of students in the learning environment.

Coaching and therapy are two other areas that have received a recent boost from positive psychology. Although these two professions are distinct from one another, practitioners of both now have a variety of positive interventions and assessments to draw upon when helping clients. Coaching, with its emphasis on positive change and optimal functioning, is a natural bed-fellow of positive psychology, and coaches can find much in the research literature relevant to their practices. Similarly, psychotherapists and counsellors are beginning to see the benefit of a solutions-focus approach to their work. New positive coaching and therapy paradigms, such as Michael Frisch's *Quality of Life Therapy and Coaching*,[9] are increasingly receiving empirical support for their effectiveness.

Perhaps one of the best aspects of positive psychology is that it brings with it its own scientific stamp of approval. Positive psychology is perfect for clients or supervisors that are wary of new and untested approaches to work. The scientific angle of positive psychology can also be useful to consultants and others who are pitching these interventions to sceptical clients. At last, there is hard evidence in the form of published peer reviewed studies you can point to as you tick off the virtues and promises of positive psychology.

Further Scepticism about Positive Psychology

Of course, not everyone is swayed by fancy statistical analyses and lofty sounding professional journals. There are many folks who still wonder—understandably—

whether positive psychology is just a passing fad. Might positive psychology be a cult, centred on the charismatic figure of Martin Seligman? Might the whole movement be too…. American? Is happiness really a serious enterprise, and one worthy of our professional interest? As both a subjective well-being (happiness) researcher and positive psychology trainer I have heard these concerns voiced around the globe in workshops, seminars, and panel discussions. I believe they are valid questions, and I – myself—would be sceptical of a positive psychology that did not take the time to address them. I am, therefore, pleased to announce that these are concerns that can largely be put to rest. I would not waste your time here if I thought positive psychology was a flavour-of-the-month discipline or that it did not transcend national boundaries.

If you are looking for evidence of positive psychology's long-lastingness, then it makes sense to seek out positive psychology institutions—those that have the promise of outlasting Martin Seligman and enduring long into the future. Fortunately, there are many examples of these. For example, positive psychology educational programs have sprung up around the globe:

- In 2005, the University of Pennsylvania established a Master in Applied Positive **Psychology degree: http://www.sas.upenn.edu/cgs/graduate/mapp/**
- The University of East London offers the same degree to people on the other side of the Atlantic Ocean:
  http://www.uel.ac.uk/psychology/programmes/postgraduate/positive-msc.htm.
- More recently, Claremont Graduate University, in California, began offering the world's first doctorate degree in positive psychology:
  http://www.cgu.edu/pages/4571.asp
- And in addition, courses on positive psychology are now being offered in dozens of universities around the world.

In addition, there are now journals dedicated to positive psychology and positive psychology topics, including:

- *Journal of Positive Psychology*
  http://www.tandf.co.uk/journals/titles/17439760.asp
- *Journal of Happiness Studies*
  http://www.springer.com/social+sciences/quality+of+life+research/journal/10902

There are also international networks of positive psychology, including:

- International Positive Psychology Association - **www.ippanetwork.org**
- European Network for Positive Psychology - **http://www.enpp.org/**
- International Society for Quality of Life Studies - **www.isqols.org.**

In addition, there are now a number of organisations devoted to the dissemination and application of positive psychology, including:

- Centre for Applied Positive Psychology (CAPP) - **www.cappeu.org**
- Centre for Confidence and Well-Being -
  http://www.centreforconfidence.co.uk/index.php

Further, there are also large research prizes (as much as a quarter of a million dollars!), research grants, regular conferences on at least four continents, and strong corporate sponsorship for positive psychology. Because professional organisations, conferences, and scientific journals are dynamic by nature, I recommend you take the initiative to search for new sources that might have sprung up since the publication of this text. Regardless of minor revisions the take-home message is clear: it looks like positive psychology is on the rise, and is here to stay.

Let me reiterate that I believe it is especially in the long term interests of positive psychology that the discipline now crosses international boundaries. The voices of researchers, managers, and practitioners from around the globe now offer a crucial cross-cultural perspective on the topic that might otherwise have gotten lost. There is a thriving European network of positive psychology enthusiasts, and the discipline is taking root in Australia, as well as smaller but vibrant groups in South America, Africa, and Asia. The cross-national discourse on the topic helps ensure that positive psychology is not simply an American discipline, and that it is adapted to be locally appropriate to widely different cultures.

One of the most dynamic aspects of positive psychology is the sense of excitement about this topic. For many people who have seen it work firsthand, positive psychology is a breath of fresh air. As a student in a distance learning course it would be a shame for you to miss out on the sense of being plugged into a wider community of people who share your interest in this topic. I want you to understand positive psychology as a widespread phenomenon and experience it as a larger whole. As such, I recommend that you spend some time on-line this first week getting to understand, firsthand, how large and fascinating positive psychology is.

1.2 Exercise

Visit the Positive Psychology Centre website (**http://www.ppc.sas.upenn.edu**), joining the friends of Positive Psychology List Serve (**http://lists.apa.org/cgi-bin/wa.exe?SUBED1=FRIENDS-OF-PP&A=1**), visiting the European Network for Positive Psychology website (**http://www.enpp.org/**), or reading the Positive Psychology News Daily (**http://pos-psych.com/**). Write brief notes below about what you found out at each of these resources:

Each of these on-line sources will give you a sense that there are other people as passionate about the topic as I am (and hopefully you are). It is my great hope that you become inspired by the enthusiasm for this subject you see in me, other researchers, and other professionals using this information in their daily work. Inspiration that I hope you carry forward into the coming weeks.

Review of Main Points from Week 1

1. Positive psychology is a new field that is concerned with mental health, strengths, positive emotions, positive institutions, and optimal functioning.

2. Positive psychology is a science and is, therefore, built on a foundation of careful study and empirical evidence.

3. Research results suggest that there is as much, or more, to be gained from capitalizing on strengths and positivity as there is from trying to overcome weaknesses. This finding applies to a number of domains ranging from business to education.

4. Positive psychology is more than a passing fad. A number of lasting institutions such as graduate education programmes, research grants, and professional journals suggest that positive psychology is enduring.

What You Will Get Out of this Course

This course will introduce you to a wide range of foundational topics in positive psychology. First, we will cover positive psychology interventions (Week 2), in which you will learn about empirically tested interventions and when they work best. In Week 3 we will address the emotional Holy Grail of happiness, and discuss how to get it and why it is one of the most important resources your clients and employers are overlooking. In Week 4 we will move on to strengths, and will learn about an exciting new assessment for tapping signature strengths, and how best to employ them at work. In Week 5 we will cover hope and optimism, and will learn how to promote both, and what that will buy us. Finally, in Week 6, we will integrate all of these exciting areas, and assess how far you've come. You will be surprised how much you have learned in such a short time!

Specific skills and knowledge you will gain from this course include:

- How to use research evidence to make a case for positive psychology;

- How and when to best apply empirically supported positive psychology interventions;

- The many benefits of positive emotion;

- How to use a new strengths assessment to guide your work;

- How to increase hope, and why you ought to;

- How to keep abreast of new developments in positive psychology.

1.3 Looking Ahead

As you look ahead to the coming weeks, it makes sense to take some time and set some educational goals for yourself, so that you have something to work toward, and something additional by which to measure your progress. Please take a moment and answer the following questions:

What attracted you to positive psychology?

What, specifically, are you curious about related to positive psychology? That is, what would you like to learn?

What scepticism or concerns do you harbour about positive psychology?

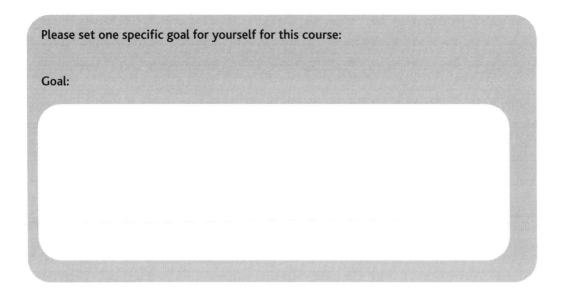

Please set one specific goal for yourself for this course:

Goal:

Reading for Week 1

Peterson, C. (2006). *A primer in positive psychology*. New York: Oxford University Press.

Please read Chapters 1 and 2.

As you read these introductory chapters you should bear in mind that Chris Peterson, the author, is not merely a reporter on the topic, he is also a member of the positive psychology steering committee. That means that he has been involved in the inner circle of some of the most exciting developments in the field from its very beginnings. There are two points in particular I like from the reading this week. The first is the section that asks, "Is positive psychology anything more than what my Sunday school teacher knows?" This is a legitimate question, and one that must be addressed honestly, openly, and effectively, by anyone hoping to use positive psychology in a professional capacity. The final answer, as you will see, is that—yes—positive psychology produces many insights that are counter-intuitive, generalisable, and otherwise beyond the scope of simple common sense. The other point Peterson makes that I think is particularly relevant to this course is that "learning about positive psychology is not a spectator sport." I would like to disabuse you of the idea that his book, or this course, is best taken in as passive reading material. In fact, I would argue, as Peterson does, exactly the opposite. The tools and techniques of positive psychology are so universally relevant, and often so powerful, that they must be experienced rather than viewed. I encourage you to approach this course as a highly interactive endeavour; one in which you will read, reflect, write, wonder, question, challenge, and apply. I firmly believe that you will benefit the most from this course if you engage with it as a highly interactive tool, approaching the exercises with seriousness and giving these concepts the depth of thought they are due.

Key References from Week 1

1. Baumeister, R. F., Bratslavsky, E., Finkenaeur, C., & Vohs, K. (2001). Bad is stronger than good. *General Review of Psychology, 5,* 323-370.
2. Maslow, A. (1954). *Motivation and personality.* New York: Harper.
3. Clifton, D. & Harter, J. K. (2003). Investing in strengths. In K. S. Cameron, J. S. Dutton, & R. E. Quinn, (Eds), *Positive organizational scholarship: Foundations of a new discipline,* (pp. 111-121). San Francisco, CA: Berrett- Koehler Publishers.
4. Kim Berg, I. & Szabo, P. (2005). *Brief coaching for lasting solutions.* New York: Norton.
5. Linley, A. & Page, N. (2007). Playing to one's strengths. *HR Director* (April).
6. Lyubomirsky, S., King, L., & Diener, E. (2005). The benefits of frequent positive affect: Does happiness lead to success? *Psychological Bulletin, 131,* 803-855.
7. As # 3
8. As # 3
9. Frisch, M. (2006). *Quality of life therapy: Applying a life satisfaction approach to positive psychology and cognitive therapy.* Hoboken, NJ: Wiley.

Further Reading

1. Seligman, M.E.P. (2002). *Authentic Happiness: Using the new positive psychology to realise your potential for lasting fulfillment.* New York: Free Press.
2. Rath, T. & Clifton, D. O. (2004). *How full is your bucket? Positive strategies for work and life.* New York: Gallup Press.
3. Special Issue of *American Psychologist* (Vol. 55, Issue 1) on Positive Psychology, January 2000.
4. Linley, P. A., Joseph, S., Harrington, S., & Wood, A. M. (2006). Positive psychology: Past, present, and (possible) future. *Journal of Positive Psychology, 1,* 3-16.

Week Two: The Power of Positive Emotion

Last week you were introduced to the general topic of positive psychology. We explored some of the historical traditions upon which it is founded and talked about how it has evolved in modern times. Among the most important take-home messages from last week are :

1) Positive psychology is a much needed adjunct to traditional psychology because it asks about happiness, optimism, strengths, and other topics that are relevant to everyday people;
2) Positive psychology is a science, and is distinguished by its heavy emphasis on high quality research;
3) There is evidence that shows a strengths-focus and attention to the positive can produce important gains in education, business, and personal life.

The Power of Emotions

Take a moment and think about the last time you had an intense emotional experience. Perhaps it was an angry outburst at a spouse, chronic irritation while stuck in rush hour traffic, or deep feelings of pride for a child's achievement. Maybe you felt excited and enthusiastic watching a sporting event, or perhaps you felt a sense of peace while tending the garden on a weekend afternoon. Our range of emotion is nothing short of amazing. What's more, emotions seem to have some almost magical properties. They are, for example, contagious. You can probably recall an instance when a friend was startled, and their reaction startled you. Maybe it is easy to remember a time that one person in a group was tickled by a funny thought and before long everyone was laughing. Emotions also seem to be linked to memory, and can be called forth by triggers such as old photographs. It turns out that feelings play an enormous but often overlooked part in our daily lives. In fact, emotions are useful, powerful, and beneficial. In short, it is worth understanding emotions—and especially the power of positive emotions— because they can be harnessed for success in all walks of life. In fact, I will tell you now: positive emotion is one of the greatest resources you and your clients, colleagues, or students are currently overlooking.

2.1 Exercise: Emotion & Memory

Take out a photo album you have not looked at in a long time. Perhaps it is a childhood album, or a wedding album, or images from a holiday trip. Spend time looking at the images and pay attention to your feelings. Pay attention to physiological reactions in your body. Are you smiling? Relaxed? Sitting upright? Pay attention, also, to the way in which your emotions shift. Do they change rapidly? Are they relatively constant? Are they easy to identify or do they seem to be a blend of feelings? Feel free to write down your insights about your feelings:

For as prevalent and powerful as emotions are, they have not always enjoyed the best reputation. For the ancient Greeks, especially the Stoic philosophers, feelings represented the lower, animalistic side of human nature. It was, according to these great thinkers, self-control and the ability to override emotion that set humans apart from other species. The ability to think rationally and overcome emotion became known as a virtue, and this notion holds sway with many people to this day. The process of morality itself was viewed as a cognitive intellectual process in which people weighed rules, norms, and values in their heads before making decisions or acting out. The intellectual legacy of them can be seen in everyday life. You have probably counselled friends to "think things through clearly," "keep your head," "be rational," and to avoid "getting worked up." These common phrases betray the underlying assumption that, for many people, feelings are distractions, obstacles to good decision making, and often lead people astray. Rationality: one point, Emotions: zero. This same cynical view of emotions can especially be seen in the case of positive feelings, which are often regarded as naïve, shallow, or selfish. Gustave Flaubert said "To be stupid, selfish, and have good health are three requirements for happiness; though, if stupidity is lacking, all is lost." Marcel Proust, the famous pessimist, was also sceptical of good feelings. He wrote, "Happiness serves hardly any other purpose than to make unhappiness possible."

Another place emotions get a bad rap is in psychological mood disorders such as depression and anxiety. Depression and other such maladies are talked about openly and frequently featured in the media. Most folks are familiar with the rising rates of depression and the use of anti-depressant medication. Although psychological problems are painful, and deserve to be treated, they carry with them a hidden message: emotions can get out of control. Many people mistakenly think of depression and anxiety as feelings that have snowballed to unwieldy proportions. As such, it only makes sense that emotions—especially negative ones such as guilt and anger—must be guarded against. Most of us, at one time or another, fall into the trap of being prejudiced against emotion. It is as if feelings were a type of Pandora's box, out of which an uncontrollable swarm of emotion will flow and pollute our lives.

2.2 Reflection

What do you think about emotions, and where do these beliefs come from?

1. What prejudices might you hold against emotions, or what might you find appealing about them? Take a moment and think about how "emotional" a person you are. Where do you think you learned these affective trends? How does the culture in which you live play in to the way you express feelings? How does your primary relationship factor in? How might your family of origin have influenced your emotionality? Feel free to write down your answer:

With so much bad press, it might be worth taking a step back and considering the merits of scepticism about emotion. It makes sense to ask, "Why do we have feelings?" What benefits could they confer if they are so primal and dangerous, if they so easily cause us problems? Are emotions like psychological tails, little pieces of our evolutionary history of which we have yet to rid ourselves? Are they a type of affective appendix, useless little organs that pose the threat of bursting at any moment? Or, could emotions be more like thumbs.... Highly adaptive and useful? It turns out that emotions, for all their potential problems, *are* useful, and understanding how best to use them can make them work for you as a resource.

What are Emotions For?

If big toes are for balance, tongues are for tasting, and hands are for grasping, then what possible use could our feelings have? Emotions, it turns out, serve many vital purposes. They are linked to our ability to remember, our ability to learn, and our ability to communicate with others. In fact—although it would dismay the Stoics - emotions are even implicated in the process of morality, with felt sentiments offering an affective guide to what we think is right or wrong. One of the most basic functions of emotion is to act as a tracking system for our lives. As you go about your daily life the interactions, circumstances, behaviours, and decisions of your day are accompanied by a wide range of emotional consequences. Emotions, when looked at this way, can be seen as information, or feedback. When you are feeling badly, that is your emotional tracking system alerting you to the fact that something is wrong in your life and needs to be attended to and perhaps corrected. When you are feeling good, your tracking system is sounding the all clear, and you are free to relax and enjoy yourself. To be sure, these tracking systems are not perfect. All of us have experienced mis-reading our environment. We occasionally misinterpret what a friend says and get angry, jump to conclusions about the motives of the driver who cut us off, are threatened by an empty dark street when there is no real cause, or feel down in the dumps for no particular reason at all. Yes, moods do not give us flawless feedback, but they are correct—surprisingly so—the vast majority of the time.

You may also have noticed that emotions also carry *motivational* consequences. When you feel badly, for example, it isn't just that you are aware of something being amiss, you often feel compelled to deal with it. If you are feeling guilty, for example, this is your emotional system warning you that you are violating your own values system, and that unpleasant feeling encourages you to correct your actions. Stealing out of the office petty cash might leave you a bit richer, but also feeling awful about yourself (hopefully). In this instance, feelings act like an internal judicial system that helps regulate behaviour. Other moods, such as fear or sadness, have similar motivational consequences. Fear, for example, compels us to avoid threatening situations, such as dark car parks. "Listening to your feelings" often means making a change in behaviour in response to them.

The function of emotion is especially easy to see in the case of negative emotions. This is a term psychologists use to describe those usually unpleasant feelings such as anger, sadness, guilt, fear, and related emotions. We feel angry when somebody has trampled on our rights, and we are moved to stand up for ourselves, even if it sometimes means lashing out. When we are sad, it tells us that we have experienced a disappointment or loss. When we are fearful, our feelings can be a powerful motivator to protect ourselves. Can you imagine how dysfunctional a world would be in which nobody felt anger, guilt, or sadness? It would be terrible! People would lie, hurt, and steal without remorse. They would let others walk all over them and tolerate injustice. And they would not be particularly moved if their dream job fell through or their spouse died. In short, without negative emotions, people would cease to function effectively. From an evolutionary point of view, negative emotions narrow our possible thoughts and actions. When we are confronted with a threat or problem, it is an evolutionary advantage to be able to act quickly, and our emotions help this process by limiting our possible response options. You have undoubtedly experienced this for yourself when you have become enraged. Rarely, in these cases, do most of us consider every possible alternative and consequence. We simply act.

It should be said, that people don't always make the best choices. Anger often leads to blurting out hurtful words that cannot be taken back, and fear sometimes keeps us from taking the kinds of risks that would ultimately lead to success. It is here, of course, that emotions earn some of their bad reputation. Even so, it is better to have a working emotional system that leads to occasional mistakes than to have none at all! Dismissing emotions on the basis of occasional faults is really a case of throwing out the baby with the bathwater. It should also be said that emotion systems as a whole (rather than discrete individual emotions) do not always function properly. For some folks, for a variety of reasons, emotions can be problematic, and this is usually where we see clinically significant problems with depression and anxiety. For some people there are biological and genetic factors that hinder effective functioning. For others the events of their lives are so painful that the emotion system is simply overwhelmed. Again, these instances are serious, and should be treated; but not because emotions are inherently dangerous but because they can be so painful or overwhelming. For the majority of people, however, emotions work just fine. It is, in part, because our feelings come in so handy that our families, businesses, and societies can function as well as they do.

2.3 Reflection: Expressing your feelings

How do you tend to express emotion? Would your friends describe you as emotional, or stoic? Are there certain types of feelings, like sadness, that you are comfortable with, and others, such as anger, that you are less comfortable with? Feel free to take the time to consider these questions in earnest and to write down your answers:

But, what about positive emotions? What can they do for us? If negative emotions are an evolutionary advantage, what use are good feelings? Positive emotions, interestingly, have been largely overlooked by psychologists. After World War II, many psychologists were interested in treating the pressing problems of trauma and other battlefield-related psychological maladies. Psychology then developed as a largely clinical discipline and emphasis was placed on negative emotions. Even now, a review of the research on emotions shows that studies on negative emotions outnumber those on positive emotions by as much as 25 to 1! Surely, good feelings are no fluke. They ought to be good for something. Or, might they just be the absence of bad feelings?

Early research on positive emotions by Alice Isen began providing some interesting new insights into the possible functions of good feelings. In a now classic study Isen and her colleagues placed coins in telephone booths.[1] Then, when unsuspecting callers had the "good fortune" of finding free money, Isen recorded how this burst of positive feeling affected them. She had an accomplice walk by and "drop some books." Oops! In the instances where callers had found money they were far more likely to help the stranger pick up the books! Although only a preliminary test, it appeared that positive emotions might be good for something, they might be associated with helping behaviours. In a more recent study, Isen and her colleagues gave small bags of chocolate (or candy, to use the US term) to medical doctors.[2] The physicians, presumably delighted with their little gift, showed significantly better diagnostic ability, and were more careful in their approach than their colleagues who had not received chocolate! Isen's groundbreaking work set the stage for the idea that positive emotion is functional. Despite her admirable work, though, it is difficult to see exactly what that function might be. If anger and guilt have clear motivational and behavioural consequences, then what might happiness lead to?

It was researcher Barb Fredrickson, now at the University of North Carolina, who advanced an elegant explanation of the power of positive emotion. If negative feelings serve to narrow our thoughts and actions, she reasoned, perhaps positive emotions broaden them. Her subsequent research showed this to be true. In her "Broaden and Build" theory of positive emotion, Fredrickson argues that feeling good broadens our interests and helps build our capabilities.[3] If negative emotions, from an evolutionary standpoint, are designed to help us deal with threats and problems in the present, positive emotions help us to prepare to deal with them in the future. Good feelings are an indicator that nothing is going wrong, and that we are free to pursue interests, pleasures, and hobbies. Interestingly, positive emotions make us more curious and interested, and more likely to try new activities and develop new skills. Positive emotions also make people more creative and better problem solvers. Positive emotions further make people more sociable, and it is when we are feeling good that we seek out others, cultivate relationships, and help people. Finally, positivity appears to "undo" the effects of negative emotions, such as helping people return more quickly to normal pulse rates and blood pressure after feeling stressed. Social alliances, creativity, skills, curiosity, and health would all be tremendous adaptive advantages.

In addition to Fredrickson's work on the topic, researcher John Cacioppo has conducted studies on the electrical impulses in facial muscles.[4] His studies show that many people react to even neutral stimuli—such as a photograph of a chair—as if they are positive. He describes how this applies to an evolutionary perspective: if our ancient forebears were inclined to see neutral environments, such as a forest with no obvious threats, as positive and hospitable then they would be more likely to explore, giving them a better knowledge of the land and a healthy advantage when predators eventually arrived. Cacioppo calls the natural tendency to interpret even neutrality as good the "positivity offset," and it provides further evidence for positive emotions being advantageous.

The Broaden and Build theory of positive emotions is, arguably, one of the most important research findings to emerge from positive psychology. At long last, this line of research and theory puts positive feelings on the map as a worthwhile topic of discussion. It is a compelling counterpoint to those sceptics who dismiss happiness as naïve, selfish, or shallow. This line of cutting edge research suggests that just the opposite is true: happiness helps us function better at work and in relationships, in those areas we care about most. What's more, the promise of positive emotion is so great that a clear case can be made for their use as a resource on the road to success in almost every walk of life. That is, the function of positive emotion is not just an issue of arcane academic interest, the results from these studies can be put directly to work in the office or at home. These research findings are not just something university professors chat about in the department hallways, they are important to you! They are interesting, universally relevant, understandable, and—ultimately— usable.

Direct Benefits of Positive Emotions

For as helpful as positive emotions may seem for our cave dwelling ancestors, we must be cautious in our approach to these emotions in modern life. It is all well and good that positive emotions lead to curiosity and friendliness, but does that really justify a place for good feelings in professional life? Can we really rationalise the idea of positivity interventions for big business? It might sound like a hard sell, if you are a consultant, manager, or coach, to suggest to a CEO that what the company needs most is more smiles. And heaven forbid we talk about "happiness." Happiness, like emotions in general, has gotten something of a bad reputation. Happiness, in many people's minds, can be synonymous with dopiness, complacency, and naiveté. Critics claim that happy people are mental simpletons, unaware of the many horrors of the real world, and are basically unmotivated. Happiness has also, of late, acquired a uniquely American accent: many people associate upbeat positivity with plucky, cowboy-ish attitudes and Hollywood happy endings. But, in reality, happiness merely means pleasant feelings, and can include joy, excitement, flow and engagement, enthusiasm, and peace. People from every nation feel happy, and there are legions of happy people who are achievement oriented and well aware of the world's problems. There is now a mountain of research data that shows that happiness, and positive emotions in general, don't just feel good but are actually good for you.

Positive emotions are beneficial. Highly beneficial. Dozens of studies using a variety of samples, methods, and analyses all converge on this same point.[5] Your clients, students, or organisation may not immediately see the value of positive emotion, but it is easy to connect good feelings to outcomes they care about. There is strong research support, for instance, for positive emotions making people healthier (fewer sick days at the office!), more creative (new products and solutions!), and friendlier (more productive teams and more altruism!). Let's take, as an example, a single domain associated with the benefits of positive emotion: health. Studies show that positivity leads to lower rates of cigarette use, drug use, suicidality, fewer emergency room and hospital visits, fewer automobile fatalities, lower blood pressure, fewer heart attacks, more physical exercise, better immune system functioning, better longevity and mortality rates, higher pain thresholds, better cardiovascular functioning, and better global health! There are similar benefits to people's social and work lives as well. Happy folks, just to give a few examples, tend to be more likely to get married, stay married, have more friends, feel more social support, help colleagues more, show up to work on time, take fewer sick days, receive better supervisor and customer evaluations, and make more money! These findings have shown up in longitudinal, experimental, and cross-sectional studies conducted by dozens of researchers with extremely varied samples. The best single source for you to see these is a 2005 article by Sonya Lyubomirsky, Laura King, and Ed Diener published in *Psychological Bulletin*. Here is a brief summary:

A sample of the many benefits of positive emotion

Health

1 Positive people are less likely than negative people to develop a cold, and when they did the symptoms were far less severe.
2 Positive nuns survived longer than their negative counterparts.
3 Depression linked to smoking, drinking, drug abuse, suicide, stroke, slower recovery rates from illnesses, and more emergency room visits.
4 Positivity linked to less pain, physical symptoms, fewer hospital visits.
5 People in a good mood have faster cardiovascular recovery times.

Social

1 Good relationships associated with better health and mental health.
2 Happiest 10% are more sociable, have stronger friendships, and romantic relationships.
3 Positive people volunteer more and are more willing to help others.
4 Positive people are more extroverted, have better club attendance, and are less selfish.

Work

1 Positivity is associated with:
   - higher salaries;
   - better supervisor evaluations;
   - better customer evaluations;
   - less absenteeism;
   - less employee turnover;
   - better organisational behaviour;
   - better relationship with colleagues.
2 Negativity costs the US economy between 250-300 billion dollars a year in lost productivity from disengaged workers.

Personal

1 Positive emotions increase interest and curiosity.
2 Positive emotions are associated with feeling more meaning in life.
3 Positive emotion leads to more creativity.

One of the great advantages of positive psychology being a science— rather than a philosophy, cult, or fad— is that it provides empirical support for longstanding claims. It is one thing to walk into the board room and suggest a happiness intervention on the factory floor, and quite another to be able to point to the 2005 article written by Sonja Lyubomirsky and her colleagues that reviews this vast body of research literature. In fact, you can tie positivity directly to outcomes that executives and managers really care about: productivity, turnover, and organisational citizenship. The science of positive psychology tells us that understanding and harnessing positive emotions is worthwhile. In fact, and I will repeat myself here: positive emotions are so widely beneficial that they may be the greatest single resource you and your clients (or students, etc.) are overlooking. If the old conceptualization of happiness is that it is a blissful emotional state that we achieve, a kind of affective finish line, then the new way of thinking can be summarized as follows: happiness is a resource, a type of emotional currency that can be spent on the other outcomes in life we care about.

Despite the strong support for this conclusion it still makes sense to tailor the language you use when talking about this topic so that it is appropriate to your profession. The word "happiness" might not fly in an organisational setting, but "better team productivity," "lower turnover," and "better conflict resolution ability" will get the attention of nearly all managers and executives. If happy faces, smiling, and laughter sound like dubious board room topics then consider "sustained cold calling capacity for the sales team," "enhanced team creativity," or "increased customer loyalty." It is important that you know your market or your client so that you can understand their values and needs and modify your language accordingly. If you work in coaching, psychotherapy, education, or human resources the fact that positive emotions are beneficial can be equally useful to you. Because good relationships, creativity, engagement, and health are universally important, the idea of harnessing the power of good feelings is relevant to all professions.

The Fundamental Question: How do We Increase Positivity?

It is a simple matter to point at good moods and say they are good for you. It is much more difficult to put practices, routines, and culture in place that support positivity. Psychotherapy clients come to us precisely because they have difficulty with positivity, coaching clients are often stymied by setbacks, classroom culture can turn competitive, and organisational culture can be a breeding ground of anxiety and despair. No doubt, promoting positivity is no simple task. Still, it can be done, and done well. Organisations have long made attempts at infusing a bit of positivity around the edges. Take the example of motivational posters that hang prominently on walls proudly announcing "Teamwork!" or "Success!" Picture the idea of "casual dress Fridays." Think, "Employee of the Month" programmes or special recognition dinners. These are all interventions aimed at making organisational culture positive and appealing. Although well-intentioned, these approaches do not always work.

It is worth considering how you already make your life more positive, both at home and at work. There are a variety of "natural" ways to increase positivity. The most obvious example is humour. Humour is not idle; it is a wonderful tonic and actually serves many purposes. Humour can dispel tense situations, bring people closer together, address difficult subjects, and be pleasurable. Engaging in humour—everything from jokes to "ice-breakers" at meetings—has long been used to get groups to cooperate and be open to learning new things. But being funny is not natural to everyone, and it might be difficult to put out an office memo to laugh more (in fact, it is just these types of well-intentioned and poorly thought through memos that are the butt of some very funny jokes!).

2.4 Reflection:
Your Past Positivity Successes

A) Take a moment and consider your home life. How do you increase the positivity at home, or within your family? Do you use praise? Recreation? Gifts? Humour? What about the physical layout of your house? Have you made changes to your décor or furniture arrangement that you feel have made a difference to how positive the atmosphere is? How do plants and lighting affect your mood? Feel free to jot down some of your answers here:

B) Now, consider your work environment and ask yourself the same types of questions. How have you contributed to a more positive culture at the office? How have your co-workers done the same? Can you think of ill-fated attempts to instil positivity? What went wrong? Where do you see a need or opportunity to make things lighter or more upbeat? Feel free to write down your answers:

The truth is, promoting positivity is complex, and success in doing it will be dependent on the particular environment in which you work. There is no cookie-cutter solution to creating a positive culture. There are, however, some basic steps that will help you along the way. First, cultural change nearly always has to begin with leadership. If you are a therapist you must model positivity for your clients, if you are a manager you must be positive in your interactions with your employees. In addition, there are empirically tested interventions that have come out of positive psychology that can be of help. So, too, can the positive psychology research on strengths, and hope and optimism be of use. These topics will all be covered in the coming weeks. Taken together, a belief in the power of positivity, the effectiveness of positive interventions, a strengths-based focus, and increasing optimism will offer you the best shot at inspiring, motivating, and engaging the people you work with. Before we rush to the how-to of increasing positivity, let's take a moment this week to understand what emotions are for, what they can do for us, and how positive emotions can work to our advantage.

Review of Main Points from Week 2

- Emotions serve a specific purpose. They help us function by providing useful feedback about our lives.

- Positive emotions, in particular, serve to broaden and build many of our resources.

- Happiness is a worthwhile topic: positivity is directly linked to social, personal, health, and work benefits.

- Positivity can be increased.

Reading for Week 2

Peterson, C. (2006). *A primer in positive psychology*. New York: Oxford University Press.

Please read Chapters 3 and 4.

In this week's reading, Chris Peterson presents a broad discussion of pleasure and positive emotion, as well as theories of happiness and scientific research on happiness. I would like to point out two items that might be of particular interest to you. First, Peterson's discussion of the research on peak-end theory. This theory says, essentially, that when we remember past emotional experiences we do not mentally tally up every moment of that experience. Instead, we give extra weight to the most intense (peak) moment and the last (end) moment. What this means is that people virtually ignore the duration of an event (called duration neglect). In real world terms what this means is that you ultimately don't care if an enjoyable film is one hour or two hours; you will make your judgment based on an average of the most intense scene and the ending. To take a different, and perhaps more compelling example, it does not matter whether your painful colonoscopy is 45 minutes rather than 15, so long as the final moments are not very painful. This has direct implications for customer service, customer-product interface, and decision making (one week in Hawaii ought to be roughly as good as two). How might this fascinating psychological phenomenon apply to your work?

Also of particular interest is the section on flow. Flow is the state of total absorption that comes when skills and challenge are optimally balanced. Workers often experience flow when they are fully engaged in tasks. You may consider what bearing flow has on your work. Can you use this theory diagnostically? That is, if a client complains of a lack of engagement might you look to assessing the amount of challenge or skill they have? Are there ways you can help usher clients toward more flow?

Key References from Week 2

1. Isen, A. M., & Levin, P. F. (1972). The effect of feeling good on helping: cookies and kindness. *Journal of Personality and Social Psychology, 17*, 107-112.
2. Isen, A., Daubman, K. A., & Nowicki, G. P. (1987). Positive affect facilitates creative problem solving. *Journal of Personality and Social Psychology, 21*, 384-388.
3. Fredrickson, B. L. (2001). The role of positive emotions in positive psychology: The Broaden-and-Build theory of positive emotions. *American Psychologist, 58*, 218-226.
4. Ito, T. A., & Cacioppo, J. (2001). The psychophysiology of utility appraisals. In D. Kahneman, E. Diener, & N. Schwarz (Eds.), *Well-being: The foundations of hedonic psychology* (pp. 470-488). New York: Russell Sage Foundation.
5. Lyubomirsky, S., King, L., & Diener, E. (2005). The benefits of frequent positive affect: Does happiness lead to success? *Psychological Bulletin, 131*, 803-855.

Further Reading

Frisch, M. B. (2006). *Quality of life therapy: Applying a life satisfaction approach to positive psychology and cognitive therapy.* Hoboken, NJ: Wiley.

Lyubomirsky, S. (2008). *The how of happiness: A practical guide to getting the life you want.* New York: Penguin Press.

2.5 An Experiential Exercise for Week 2

Emotions are felt in the moment. As psychological experiences, a good way to gain a deeper understanding of emotion is to actually experience them! Use the exercises below to trigger your emotions and gain all new insight!

Pay attention this week to the social aspects of emotion. When you are in group situations, try to be aware of if the group is all united in their feeling or if there are multiple feelings. How do you know? What do cues such as facial expression and posture tell you? Try to pay attention to when and how humour, positivity, compliments, pride, and joy are used socially. How do you use them in a group situation? How do other people use them, if they use them in a way different from yours?

Week Three: Empirically tested interventions

Stop me if you've heard this one:

A woman holding a baby gets onto a bus and the driver says, "Lady, that is the ugliest thing I have ever seen!" The woman, obviously, is taken aback. Speechless and flustered, she pays her fare and takes her seat. The man in the seat next to her leans over and says, "I heard what the bus driver just said and I think it was incredibly rude! You should go up there and give him a piece of your mind. Here, I'll hold your monkey….."

Although this is far from the funniest joke in the world (but my kids love it) it is a nice example of how easy creating positivity can be. Jokes, witty banter, cartoons, friendly teasing, comedies at the theatre and cinema, our world is naturally full of feel-good interventions. If you need further proof just smile at someone as you walk down the street. Of course, they won't always smile back, but often they do. Want a bigger emotional pay-off? Try paying the toll of the person in the car behind you on your daily commute! It can take surprisingly little to boost a person's mood, including your own.

Positive psychology has produced good theory and practical applications about positive interventions. That is, the profession has now extended beyond the "easy steps," "secrets," and peppy talk of the self-help movement. Admittedly, some of the advice given in self-growth seminars and self-help books is sound and effective, but positive psychology brings a new level of rigor to the enterprise of increasing positivity. Scientists are able to test interventions to see which ones appear to be most effective, for whom, and why. In addition, positive psychology interventions are not solely about making individuals happier….while I hope last week's content went a long way toward convincing you that individual happiness is incredibly important to functioning families, workplaces, and societies, it is short sighted to only look at the individual. Positive psychology interventions have also focused on group and organisational strategies. I hope that both individual and organisation level interventions will help you work with students and clients to enable them to function even better.

What is a Positive Intervention?

James Pawelski, who administers the landmark Master of Applied Positive Psychology (MAPP) program at the University of Pennsylvania, teaches a course called "Positive Interventions," in which he asks the basic question: what are they? Are positive interventions practices we engage in to achieve desirable outcomes? In that case therapy for depression could be considered a positive intervention. Or physical exercise could be a positive intervention. In fact, nearly every activity from attending a language class to learning a new computer program to cheering up a friend would be a positive intervention under this definition. Alternately, could we define positive interventions as tools that use only distinctly *positive* methods? Here we might distinguish between a coach yelling at his players by way of encouragement versus praising them in an effort to motivate. In this instance, there is something positive, something friendly, warm, or values consistent that is the hallmark of positive interventions. As you can see, the answer to the question of what constitutes such interventions is not immediately clear, and discussion of an accurate definition can be helpful.

Pawelski suggests that **positive interventions are unique in that they are aimed at *optimal* functioning rather than just functioning**. He uses a metaphor to explain: imagine a person recovering from surgery and visiting a physical therapist. This therapist has the client engage in physical activity with the goal of recovering "normal" functioning. In other words, taking the patient from a negative to a zero point. Now, think about a person visiting a personal trainer at a gym. The trainer engages in many of the same activities, running the client through repetitive physical exercise, but this time with the aim of taking an already healthy body and making it perform even better. In this case the emphasis is on shifting from a zero point, or mildly positive point to an even more extreme positive point. Positive interventions, according to Pawelski, are defined more by their focus than their method. Positive interventions are those that focus on optimal, rather than normal functioning.

Pawelski offers another interesting insight into using techniques to promote positivity. This second point relates to a problem versus solution focus. Again, he uses a metaphor to clarify the issue: If you were magically granted super powers like a hero in a comic book, but could have only one of two kinds, which would you choose? The first type would be the power to fight problems such as battling crime and saving people from earthquakes. The second type would be the power to promote positives. Here you would have the power to keep kids in school, keep families happy, and keep workers engaged. Take a minute and really try to appreciate the difference between these two sets of powers. Which would you choose? If you are anything like me you would lean toward dealing with problems, you would want to directly address the suffering associated with problems and you can see immediate benefit. There is no shame in this choice….. it turns out that problems are more immediate and feel more pressing. They tend to attract our attention. Interestingly, the second type of power has longer term benefits and will help equip people with the ability to deal with their own problems as they arise. Pawelski's thought experiment exposes two points: First, that **dealing with *both* problems and solutions are superior to focusing on either one alone; and second, that promoting positivity is highly worthwhile**. Fortunately, positive psychologists have begun testing various techniques and now have a preliminary toolbox for increasing positivity. We now have, if you will, a whole new set of super powers.

3.1 Reflection: Positivity in Your Own Life

Consider a time when you felt helped by another person. Perhaps it was during a troubled period or when you had experienced a frustration or set-back. Maybe it was related to a personal issue such as a friendship problem or a health concern. Possibly it was related to the workplace.....perhaps you felt you had failed at an important objective or were having difficulty with a co-worker. Maybe it was something seemingly minor provided for you by a stranger. Regardless of the specific helper or type of help what was it that gave you the boost you needed to power through that difficult time? Feel free to write down your initial thoughts here:

Now, look over your answer. Consider how complete it is. As I suggest other mechanisms that may have been instrumental in helping you at that time— encouragement, a new point of view, a boost of self-confidence, hope to go on, the use of new resources, a tip or piece of advice, a tool for some new behaviour or activity—please re-consider your answer above. We often overlook how complex the help we receive is, and on how many different levels it works. As you re-think your answer, what would you add? What else was instrumental about the help that was provided to you? Please write down you thoughts here:

Now, think again about that time. There was likely a problem, and the help was likely associated with a solution. Think about *how* the help was offered. How was it framed? Did you or the helper focus on removing or overcoming the problem? Did you simply see a new way of getting to the desired outcome, by-passing the problem entirely? Was there more talk of problems or more talk of solutions? Where was your focus, and where was the focus of the helper? Feel free to write down your answers here:

Empirically Supported Interventions

For years, religious leaders, coaches, and self-help gurus have been trying to steer us toward the things we want in life: morality, success, health, recognition, and happiness, among others. They have dispensed advice ranging from "think positively" to "write down your goals." But, do these goals work? Sure, some of them do. The problem is, this kind of advice has traditionally been given in a formulaic way, as if these methods ought to work equally well for every individual. In addition, there is plenty of advice out there that is not effective, and which is largely the product of faddish philosophies or only loosely based on scientific findings (I point you to the example of popular diets). Positive psychology, in recent years, has been gravitating more and more toward being an applied science. No longer are we—as researchers—just concerned with mapping happiness or diagnosing character strengths, we are interested in how best to put our exciting findings to use in everyday life. Admittedly, this trend toward application is only a few years old, so we don't have 100 different empirically validated interventions. The science is young and the next few years will see more new interventions being developed and tested. That said, we do have some very good ideas about the effectiveness and limits of the handful of interventions that have already received careful scrutiny (see "interventions-at-a-glance" chart on page 60).

A few years ago Martin Seligman and his research team wrote an article that was meant to be a "positive psychology report card."[1] In it, they proudly presented data showing that there were reliable tools for decreasing depression and increasing happiness. As a quick reminder from last week, increasing happiness is far more worthwhile than it might sound because it is directly linked to health, helping behaviours, creativity, and desirable outcomes at work. One exciting finding from the Seligman research is that some of these positive psychology tools seemed to have fairly long-lasting effects, with experimental groups showing more happiness than control groups, even months after the intervention occurred. One of these interventions was identifying and using personal strengths. Remember back in week one when we talked about the Gallup research showing that workers loved the opportunity to "do what they do best every day?"[2] In fact, there is recent research from a large international sample that show that "having an opportunity to learn" and "to be at my best" are very strong predictors of happiness. Seligman's research reinforced these conclusions. Using your strengths and feeling that you are "at your best" carry tremendous benefits ranging from better performance to increased perseverance to a greater sense of meaning and engagement. Although we will discuss strengths (and strengths interventions) in depth next week, you should note here that strengths interventions have received empirical support for their efficacy. There have also been many other positive interventions that have received research attention and support for their effectiveness, some of which Sonja Lyubomirsky documents in her book *The How of Happiness* (Penguin, 2008).

1) *Expressing Gratitude.* Perhaps the best known and most widely used of all such interventions is "expressing gratitude." As the name implies this technique is just a simple way of making sure you say thank-you. In the hectic modern world we often forget to tell others how appreciative we are. One Gallup study found that 65% of Americans reported receiving *no* recognition for a job well done in the entire year preceding the poll![3] Usually, we are pretty good at remembering to praise our children, and to express formal thanks, such as sending cards in response to gifts. But, if this is the extent of our gratitude then surely we are missing many golden opportunities.

There are countless times every day that we could be acknowledging spouses, colleagues, and strangers in a powerful and authentic way. I will give you a recent example from my own life: For years, I have employed an excellent translator, Avirupa, for those times when I travel to Kolkata (formerly Calcutta) and conduct research in the slums. These communities are sometimes difficult to work in and Avirupa does a phenomenal job of gaining access, dealing with problems as they arise, and—of course—translating. As I write these words I am preparing for another research trip to Kolkata and Avirupa has outdone herself in gaining us access to a very "private" slum (they are suspicious of outsiders). When I said, "Thank you so much for the great work" Avirupa responded, "Why are you thanking me for what I am being paid to do anyway?" (sound like a familiar attitude?). My response was, "Because I am genuinely appreciative of the excellent work you have done. Because I don't think your pay check captures the full breadth of my gratitude. Because I don't believe you work only for money. Because I value you." The effect was both profound and immediate: Avirupa told me that she was more motivated than ever to work hard, that she felt great about herself, and that my comments inspired loyalty because she felt personally valued. My comments were, truthfully, a very small matter, simple to say. And yet, they had as powerful affect as any threat or job perk.

There are many ways to express gratitude. The most obvious is simply to say thank you to those people you appreciate. But, there are other means as well. The best known method, and the one that has received the greatest scientific scrutiny, has come to be called "the gratitude exercise," although some folks know it as "the three blessings exercise." Regardless of the title used, people are asked to keep a daily gratitude journal. That is, each day—usually at the same time of day so that people can better develop the habit—they record three things they are grateful for. That's all: simply write down three things to be appreciative of. These items could be as broad as "I am thankful to be alive" or as specific as "I am thankful to have a working refrigerator." Sometimes people treat themselves to fancy journals, or occasionally conduct the exercise with a spouse; whatever the specific instructions the effects of this simple exercise are powerful. People routinely report feeling more positive, more "awake" to daily life, and sometimes report better relationships with others. Seligman's research, as well as other studies, have confirmed that this is a widely effective tool.[4] Indeed, I regularly assign this activity to the students in my university positive psychology course and—of the 100 enrolees—80% or more enjoy the activity and report more positivity, and roughly 15% continue with the activity long after the assignment is over. At the end of this week's content, I am going to suggest that you keep a gratitude log for the coming week to see how it affects you.

Another variation on expressing gratitude is to write a letter of gratitude to someone who has been instrumental in helping you in some important way. This activity taps a slightly different aspect of gratitude. Rather than being thankful for on-going good work or everyday help, the gratitude letter highlights very large contributions. These are typically written to parents, coaches, mentors, teachers, or others who have had a profound impact on your development. These folks love receiving such letters, it feels fantastic to write them, and it is often fun to re-kindle an old relationship. Interestingly, writing a gratitude letter can be an emotionally powerful experience even if you do not intend to post it!

A related variation is called the "gratitude visit," and it is an in-person version of the gratitude letter. But be forewarned, actually showing up and telling someone, face-to-face, how much they have meant to you can be daunting! A while ago, I appeared on a Canadian television show where I asked 4 participants to conduct a gratitude visit. Initially, the four of them shrugged off the task, saying things like "I thank people in my life all the time!" But when push came to shove, the TV show participants found that actually sitting across from someone to whom they owed thanks was a humbling and difficult process. Like the folks on the TV show, many people find the emotional intimacy somewhat anxiety provoking. But, for those who get through that minor difficulty the story is nearly always the same: "It felt so good to finally express what I had bottled up, it brought me and X closer together, it just felt great." Whatever the specific gratitude activity, research shows that this small activity boosts happiness, and that the tonic effects of this type of journaling can last months. Some folks, like Tal Ben-Shahar, author of the book *Happier*, report that they have done this activity every day for years and still reap psychological benefits!

There are many reasons why this deceptively simple exercise might be so effective. First, humans have an extraordinary capacity to adapt to new circumstances. This gift is the reason we can get married, move to a new city, or change jobs. We tend to adjust well. Our natural adaptation allows situations and experiences to recede into the mental background to free up our psychological resources to attend to new, novel stimuli. Unfortunately, this ability to adapt has a hidden dark side: we can quickly lose the emotional thrill of novel events. The excitement of a new house, spouse, or job can dampen into a sense of routine. What was once fresh gradually becomes habitual. The gratitude exercise might serve as a psychological antidote to this process, keeping us aware of the good things around us. By exerting the effort to focus our attention on positives we can avoid the drudgery of the workaday world. Expressing gratitude then, can be seen as a kind of "mindfulness." Another reason this activity might be so effective is that it could have spill over effects. By becoming aware of even three small things to be grateful for, for instance, we might prime ourselves to pay attention to a broad array of positives. Noticing one pleasing thing about work, home, or a friendship, could set the stage for further vigilance in these categories.

3.2 Reflection: Gratitude at Work

A) Expressing gratitude might be great for husbands or appreciative students, but is it appropriate to the workplace? Take a moment and consider how you might use the various gratitude exercises, or variations thereof, in your own work. How might managers use gratitude authentically and strategically to cultivate relationships and motivate workers? How does gratitude fit in your own business model? If you are a therapist, coach, or consultant, when do you use gratitude with your clients? What is the effect? Feel free to write down your answers here:

B) Even for as powerful a tool as gratitude is, it does not come naturally to everyone nor is it the traditional way businesses have been managed. Whether you are an executive, HR professional, teacher, or therapist, think about the potential problems you foresee with introducing gratitude exercises into your workplace. How might you overcome these obstacles or frame gratitude exercises in a way that makes sense locally? Feel free to write your answers here:

2) *Positive Reminiscence.* Another intervention that has received empirical support is positive reminiscence. In this exercise, people are asked to spend time recalling a positive event from the past. This could be an occasion that brings pleasant memories, such as a wedding, or a time they are proud of, such as receiving an award at work. Fred Bryant, a researcher at the University of Chicago, has also suggested that this activity can be done with the use of physical memorabilia, such as trophies, college degrees, printed e-mails, or photographs. In his studies, Bryant shows that spending a few minutes basking in past successes or good times from long ago can boost positivity.[5] In fact, this technique has been used with executives and students to build confidence. One of the nice features of this exercise is its obvious appeal. While some folks might think that writing down blessings is hokey, most folks find the prospect of remembering their own shiniest moments attractive. One interesting variation on positive reminiscence is to create a "positive portfolio." In this exercise people gather together physical items that attest to prior success. A success paper trail if you will. Positive portfolios might contain thank you letters from students, a touching anniversary card, a photocopy of a university diploma, an acceptance letter, or other tallies of personal achievement. These portfolios can be used to boost confidence before a presentation or interview, or simply to increase positivity when it is needed.

At the heart of positive reminiscence is the psychological act of savouring. Savouring, according to Bryant, is all about taking a positive moment in time and mentally stretching it out, extending it, making it last a little bit longer.[6] Some folks naturally do this through a type of imaginary "instant-replay." Imagine, for example, that you are working with a client on a problem and you said just exactly the most helpful thing possible: it was witty, on the mark, and led directly to a solution. For the rest of the day you might replay the scene in your head, mentally patting yourself on the back for a job well done. The nice thing about savouring is that it is an internal process and, as such, we don't have to worry much about social conventions regarding humility. Positive reminiscence and savouring are different from bragging. We can appreciate our finer moments without boasting about our achievements, or even suggesting that our successes make us better than anyone else. According to Bryant, many people are natural savourers and the skill can also be learned. One method is to take a mental snap shot of a success as it happens…. Catalogue what the room looked like, who was present, how you felt, and so forth. By paying close attention to the details it will be easier to conjure specific images for later savouring.

3) *Best Possible Self.* Another effective route to positivity is the so-called "best possible self" exercise. Essentially, this activity is a combination of imagining yourself at your absolute best and the cathartic experience of free writing. This activity was born out of research showing that when people wrote in an expressive fashion, they tended to feel better.[7] Setting fears and troubles down on paper seems to be therapeutic for most folks. Extending this line of reasoning to a specifically positive approach, researcher Laura King has tested the effects of writing about one's best possible self.[8] In this exercise people are encouraged to write about their potential. But, be forewarned, if done improperly, this tool can backfire. Some people are apt to compare their current self with their optimal self, and come away feeling disappointed. Imagining a better you can, unfortunately, expose how large the gap is between the ideal and real. Usually, this negative effect results when the exercise is administered incorrectly and is easily rectified. To get around this problem, King encourages people to write about a possible "future self."

A typical instruction for this activity might read: "Imagine yourself in the future. Imagine everything has gone about as well as it could have, and that you have gotten most of the things that are important to you. Describe this life." This sets the stage for people to take stock of their values and define their aspirations. People are asked to write continually, letting their thoughts and feelings flow out. The emphasis should be on committing words to page without care for grammar or punctuation. This flow helps folks engage in this activity with less self-censorship, fewer criticisms, and less fear that their vision isn't realistic. Usually, the best possible self exercise results in a little boost of inspiration and motivation to rise to this potential. [9] The best possible self exercise might be especially appropriate to people in a new position, taking on a new project, or facing a difficult problem.

3.3 Activity: Best Possible Self Exercise

Try out the "best possible self" exercise for yourself. Set aside 10 full minutes to do this, and I recommend you get a timer or stopwatch to help you. Take time and think about your life in the future. Imagine that you have gotten most of the things you have wanted in life and performed the way you would have liked. Spend your time writing about what this life would look like. Do not worry about grammar or punctuation but rather try to pour your thoughts and feelings out onto the page in an expressive way. You will likely want to use a separate sheet (or sheets!) of paper for this exercise. Please do this exercise now.

Read this when you are finished: Now that you have finished, take time to reflect on how you feel. What is the effect of having done this exercise? To what extent is the effect emotional rather than a matter of how you see yourself or your life? Do you feel inspired or motivated? Do you feeling like making changes? How did this activity affect you? Feel free to write your answers here:

4) *Counting Kindnesses.* Although there are several other positive psychology interventions that have received some preliminary research support for their effectiveness, I will discuss only one other here: Counting kindnesses. Humans have a wonderful capacity to find meaning in life and the vast majority of folks have a clear sense of personal values. Because we are primates, and therefore social creatures, many of these values are related to helping, and not harming, others. It should come as no surprise, then, that altruism has emerged in the research literature as one of the activities that promotes well-being and positivity. Doing good deeds for family members, friends, and even strangers feels good. The chance to help another person—even if it is as simple as providing street directions— can help us connect to a sense of purpose in life, and a feeling that we are fulfilling some important moral mission. As I think back on my own life it is easy for me to bring up instances of helping others: the time the woman dropped her purse while exiting the airplane, the time I was the first person to come upon the scene of a car accident, the time I helped a man in the street having a seizure, the time I mentored a student who was later accepted at a prestigious graduate school, the time I "sponsored" a child in India….the list goes on and on. It isn't that I think I am any better, or even any more helpful, than other people. It's just that these examples still make me feel good when I reflect on them. They allow me a small sense of having lived a worthwhile life and made the world a better place in some small way. Undoubtedly, you have your own list.

3.4 Reflection: Your Kindness History

If your parents were anything like mine—and they probably were in this respect—they taught you to be kind to others. Although you might not realise it, your life is a stunning litany of kind deeds done for others. From the time you first shared a toy with a fellow toddler to the time you held the door for a stranger your life has been as series of kindnesses, large and small. Take a moment and reflect on all you have done. Don't worry, no one is watching. No one will feel like you are bragging. Give yourself permission to pat yourself on the back. Take this time to write down those examples that really stand out, the kind deeds you feel especially good about (use additional sheets of paper if you need to!):

Interestingly, one study looking at keeping track of kindnesses produced a somewhat counter-intuitive result. In this study, the researchers asked participants in the first experimental group to practice 5 small acts of kindness in a single day, and those in another group to practice the same number of kindnesses across a week.[10] Although intentionally engaging in these helping behaviours was psychologically rewarding to people in both groups, it was those who clustered their generosity in a single day who showed the greats benefits. You might think that being a little kind each day, and spreading altruism across the week would have more tonic effects, but it turns out that the more intense clustering of kindnesses produces stronger results. Notably, the researchers did not test what happens if you were to practice 5 acts of kindness every single day! This has, of course, obvious implications for psychotherapy patients, students, and the workplace. Lending a hand is a relatively easy thing to do, and the emotional payoff can be large.

Interventions at-a-glance

Name	Benefit	Personal Fit
1. Expressing Gratitude	Closer relationships, increased appreciation, increased happiness	Colleagues, managers, therapists, clients, teachers students, people who enjoy small daily assignments
2. Positive Reminiscence	Increased appreciation, increased optimism and sense of efficacy, increased positivity	Executives, teams, couples clients, people who are generally high achievers or have a positive sense of self
3. Savouring	Increased self-confidence Increased enjoyment and positivity	Everyone
4. Best Possible Self	Increased confidence and optimism, happiness	Students, clients, employees, executives, people who are aware of their strengths
5. Altruism	Increased positivity, a sense of increased meaning better relationships	Everyone
6. Using Strengths	Increased sense of meaning and engagement, increased happiness.	Everyone

Broad Interventions

Up to this point we have been discussing research support for specific tools—the positive psychology equivalents of hammers, screwdrivers, and drills— and I very much hope that these techniques can prove useful to you personally and in your work. However, although these interventions have received the positive psychology science seal of approval in the form of empirical testing, they are largely about dealing with single individuals, and in a very narrow "homework assignment" type way. Many people, especially those working in organisational settings, will be interested in broader interventions, or those that combine tools together. Whether you are a consultant or a schoolteacher, you may be interested in how positivity can be fostered at a wider level. This is, to a certain extent, the type of intervention community psychologists are interested in when they hope to improve neighbourhood involvement in planned zoning changes or launch an anti-littering campaign or reduce smoking. One important lesson from community psychology is that there is a distinction between *production* and *satisfaction* goals related to organisational change.

Production goals are those related to the mission of the organisation, such as selling magazine subscriptions, manufacturing ball-point pens, or developing cutting edge advertising campaigns. Production goals are the Hollywood stars of organisational goals because they are most obviously related to the Oscar award of business: the bottom line. When we look to change an organisation it is often production goals that get the lion's share of attention. Managers and executives consider how resources can be used differently to increase productivity, however that concept may be defined.

Satisfaction goals, on the other hand, are those related to the subjective well-being of individual employees. These goals are a little like looking at the internal health of a body, making sure all the individual organs are functioning properly and working together well. Although productivity in an organisation might surge upward for a quarter it is possible for employee satisfaction to go down at the same time.

Consider the example of a social service agency that places a premium on tracking successes, in part because their government funding depends on measurable positive results. Imagine that they pull workers out of customer service situations to work on reports showing the effectiveness of various social welfare programmes. While this new policy might be superior in tracking progress and producing well-documented successes, it risks lowering the satisfaction of the workers themselves. How so? Many people who take social service positions do so out of a desire to interact with and help others. Taking these people away from direct contact with the public they serve—removing them from the very work situation from which they draw the most meaning—is likely to lead to short-term dissatisfaction and long-term drops in productivity and rises in absenteeism and turnover. The most effective change policies are those that attend to both productivity and satisfaction goals.

There are, of course, no precise answers to the question of optimal positive organisational change as each organisation is made up of different staff and has different goals and market contexts. There is no positive formula that will work for all companies.   That said, there are a number of strong candidates for developing positive culture. First, it is important to remember the role of leaders in setting the pace of organisational change and acting as an exemplar of the new culture. If you are a coach, consultant, or manager, you are in a unique position to set the ball rolling by modelling positivity, tailoring positive interventions to teams, and creating structures for positivity. As an example of the latter, the Centre for Applied Positive Psychology, itself, has created a routine that promotes the best in its staff: positive 360s. In a positive 360 staff members come together, face-to-face, and give positive feedback to one another. They tell their colleagues what they are appreciative for, what strengths they see being played out during the work day, list their peers' successes, as well as discussing anything that they would like their colleagues to change because it is unhelpful. The result is remarkable: employees who feel valued, praised, engaged, and—perhaps—are more willing to change behaviours that are not productive.

Of course, this method would have to be tailored to be appropriate to your local work environment, and does not mean that no constructive criticism is ever given….. but rather, there is a guarantee that positive feedback will be given. In addition to leadership and modelling the idea of *autonomy-support* is crucial to positive motivation. In a nutshell, mangers who are autonomy-supportive give skilled workers lee-way to decide for themselves "how" to accomplish their goals. Board members, stock holders, and executives may decide "what" needs to get done, and "when" it ought to be completed, but most people are motivated when they have control over the "how."

Avoiding "One-size-fits-all"

The science of positive psychology is wonderful in how rapidly it has produced and validated interventions. While some folks make extraordinary claims of there being hundreds of effective positive interventions, very few of these have been tested rigorously. Of those that have, we now have preliminary proof of their efficacy. It is nice to have tools that have been empirically supported, and refreshing to learn that there is so much power in a positive focus. That said, some of the potential of positive psychology has been over-promised, or applied in too formulaic a way. Here it is worth remembering the old adage, "If your only tool is a hammer, then everything looks like a nail."

There are, sadly, many practitioners out there who blindly prescribe the gratitude exercise to each and every client, regardless of appropriateness, for the simple fact that research shows that "it works." The effectiveness of the gratitude exercises, in particular, are the most widely publicised and probably—accordingly- the most widely used by coaches, consultants, and therapists. It is not only important to know which positive interventions work, but also how to choose which intervention to use with whom.

Jordan Silberman conducted preliminary research in which he allowed coaching clients in one group to choose their own positive intervention while those in a second group were assigned (in equal proportions) to these same interventions.[11] The good news is that Silberman found that the positive interventions increased happiness and decreased depression, on average, across groups and across interventions, replicating earlier studies. Interestingly, however, there were no differences in the efficacy of the intervention based on whether it was freely chosen or assigned. This means that we still have more to learn about how best to decide between and work with positive interventions. Perhaps trial-and-error is the best we can do; perhaps it is just as well that clients select for themselves; perhaps coaches and others with expertise in positive psychology are ultimately the best judges. Positive psychology is not a one-size-fits-all approach to life. Knowing that a given intervention has received research support is different than knowing with whom it will best work, when it will best work, and why.

Positive psychologist Sonja Lyubomirsky has conducted studies that show that the idea of "fit" is very important to intervention success.[12] Rather than hammering your clients or students with cookie cutter interventions, Sonja suggests that it is prudent to consider when to optimally use them. She and her colleagues have conducted research that shows that there are a number of factors that suggest when a positive psychology intervention might, and might not, be used. Among these are motivation, person-activity fit, continued practice, and effort. That is, Lyubomirsky has found that standard positive psychology interventions work better for some people than others. For a person to really benefit, he or she has to be *intrinsically motivated* to participate in the intervention, *put in the effort* required, and *see it through* until it pays off. Perhaps more importantly, people have to *see interventions as consonant with their identities and values*. They have to believe the activity is aligned with who they are. Part of your job—whether it is coaching, consulting, or teaching—is helping the people you work with to find the links between these interventions and outcomes they value. In addition, it is helpful to be able to translate the sometimes "self-helpy" terminology of positive psychology into language your clients recognise and use. Words like happiness, gratitude, and kindness can seem too soft-headed for many people. Take the time to consider how these important concepts can be reframed in your clients' language. Kindness, for example, might easily translate to "teamwork," and gratitude might better be seen as "performance-based recognition." The more you can tailor interventions to your specific area of work, the more beneficial and effective they are likely to be.

3.5 Activity

Try translating some of the so-called "soft" terminology of positive psychology into language that will be well received by the people you work with. For each concept below think of work-appropriate synonyms:

Positive Psychology Concept   **Work-appropriate Synonyms**

1. Happiness:

2. Kindness:

3. Strengths:

4. Gratitude:

5. Hope:

Summary of Main Points from Week 3

- There are a number of empirically tested interventions that have been shown to increase positivity, decrease depression, and—perhaps—enhance creativity and productivity.

- There are a number of ways to use these exercises. Taking just the example of the powerful intervention of promoting gratitude, there are a variety of ways to apply this ranging from keeping a gratitude journal to conducting a gratitude visit. You can be creative in your implementation of positive interventions.

- Positive psychology is not one-size-fits-all. Be sure to tailor interventions so that they fit the situations and clients you work with.

Reading for Week 3

Peterson, C. (2006). *A primer in positive psychology*. New York: Oxford University Press.

Please read Chapter 11.

In this week's reading Chris Peterson offers a broad look at "enabling institutions," including positive families, schools, workplaces, and societies. While you might not find all of these sections relevant it may be interesting to note that a wide range of positive institutions are possible. For those primarily interested in workplace concerns you might want to pay special attention to the sections on institutional level values, types of authority, and types of workers.

Key References from Week 3

1. Seligman, M. E. P., Steen, T., Park, N., & Peterson, C. (2005). Positive psychology progress: Empirical validation of interventions. *American Psychologist, 60*, 410-421.
2. Clifton, D. & Harter, J. K. (2003). Investing in strengths. In K. S., Cameron, J. E. Dutton, & R. E. Quinn, (Eds), *Positive organizational scholarship: Foundations of a new discipline* (pp. 111-121). San Francisco, CA: Berrett- Koehler Publishers.
3. Rath, T., & Clifton, D. (2004). *How full is your bucket? Positive strategies for work and life*. New York: Gallup Press.

4. Emmons, R. A. (2007). *Thanks! How the new science of gratitude can make you happier*. New York: Houghton-Mifflin.

5. Bryant, F. B., Smart, C. M., & King, S. P. (2005). Using the past to enhance the present: Boosting happiness through positive reminiscence. *Journal of Happiness Studies, 6,* 227-260.

6. Bryant, F. B. & Veroff, J. (2007). *Savoring: A new model for positive experience.* Mahwah, NJ: Erlbaum.

7. Pennebaker, J.W. (1997). *Opening up: The healing power of expressing emotion.* New York: Guilford Press.

8. King, L.A. (2001). The health benefits of writing about life goals. *Personality and Social Psychology Bulletin, 27,* 798–807.

9. Lyubomirsky, S., Sousa, L., & Dickerhoof, R. (2006). The costs and benefits of writing, talking, and thinking about life's triumphs and defeats. *Journal of Personality and Social Psychology, 90,* 692-708.

10. Otake, K., Satoshi, S., Junko, T., Kanako, O., & Fredrickson, B. (2006). Happy people become happier through kindness: A counting kindnesses intervention. *Journal of Happiness Studies, 3,* 361-375.

11. Silberman, J. (2007). Positive intervention self-selection: Developing models of what works for whom. *International Coaching Psychology Review, 2,* 70-77.

12. Lyubomirsky, S. (2008). Personal communication.

Further reading

Emmons, R. A. (2007). *Thanks! How the new science of gratitude can make you happier.* New York: Houghton-Mifflin.

Lyubomirsky, S., Sousa, L., & Dickerhoof, R. (2006). The costs and benefits of writing, talking, and thinking about life's triumphs and defeats. *Journal of Personality and Social Psychology, 90,* 692-708.

Lyubomirsky, S. (2008). *The how of happiness: A scientific approach to getting the life you want.* New York: Penguin.

3.6 Reflections

We have all experienced tough times and times where everything seemed to go just right. It can be helpful to access your own personal wisdom, gained through experience, as you approach the topic of positive intervention. What interventions took place that helped you through your dark periods, and what interventions may have facilitated those times when you were flourishing?

Consider a time when you were at your absolute best. Maybe it was when you had your work and home lives balanced well. Perhaps it was a productive time at the office. What was going on for you during that period that helped you to succeed? What factors were in place that greased the wheels? Which of your personal strengths and resources were you using? What outside support did you enjoy?

3.7 Exercises

The best way to learn about the power and effectiveness of positive interventions is to experience them for yourself. In addition, by trying out interventions on yourself, you have the opportunity to practice their administration before you deliver them to your clients.

Try the 3 blessings exercise. Get yourself a journal or notebook exclusively for this purpose (have fun with it, don't just write on the back of your grocery list!). Try to write at the same time each day, so that you can more easily develop the habit. You may want to do this activity when you wake up, to give the day a positive start, or it might make sense to do it when you go to bed, so that you can take stock of the day. Each day, write down three things you are grateful for. They may be large or small. Do this assignment each day for a week, but not necessarily longer. Notice how this task affects your attention and your attitude as you go through your day. Be aware of your moods and emotions. Pay attention to the reasons why you think this exercise works, or doesn't, as the case may be.

Mid-course Assessment

Congratulations! You have arrived at the half way point. In the spirit of employing multiple avenues for learning I would like to offer you the opportunity to apply what you have learned so far. Please write paragraph-long answers to the three questions below.

1) If a friend were to say to you "why are you wasting your time studying positive psychology?" how might you— drawing on what you have learned thus far— defend your desire to do so.

2) With what you have learned in mind, please briefly describe in your own words what you think "emotions are for." That is, how might we best describe their function.

3) Please briefly discuss some advantages and limitations of positive psychology interventions.

Week Four: A Strengths Focus

Think back for moment to when you were a child. There is an experience from childhood that many of us share. Regardless of the type of education we had, most of us took some sort of compulsory physical education class. Often, these courses divided the class in half to form teams to scrimmage against one another. Whether the game was football, kickball, cricket, lacrosse or baseball the process of dividing up was usually the same. Team captains were elected or appointed and they then took turns choosing players. Invariably the best and most athletic kids were picked first, and those unfortunate children with the least talent were chosen last. The first half of the choosing ceremony focused on acquiring the strongest players, and the second half typically focused on trying to manage the careful acquisition of the weakest players, those who might cause the least amount of damage! The message was always clear: we want strengths-based teams because that will be our best shot at success. Another message also comes through: first, we look to strengths, then—when those are in play—we manage weaknesses.

This approach to sports wasn't always socially kind or fair to all the kids in class, of course, but it was a clear, well-defined strategy. And, interestingly, one that is entirely strengths based, capitalizing on the potential of a strong team. Of course we do the same thing in adulthood: we try to hire the most talented workers, marry the best partner, buy the pet with the best qualities, and hang out with the most solid friends. To some extent, all of us have experience with a strengths-focus, in one form or another.

4.1 Reflection

Before we delve too deeply into this topic, and before I start influencing your thinking about strengths by telling what positive psychologists have to say on the matter, take some time to consider your own conceptualization of strengths. Think about how you would define a strength. How does the dictionary define it? To your mind, is there an important difference between strengths, skills, talents, morals, and values? Are these concepts related? Are they words we can use interchangeably? Feel free to write your answers here:

Looking back on those childhood competitions, we realise that the ultimate focus was not in the choosing of the teams, but in the playing of the game. The real question, then, is: what happens *after* the teams are chosen? What happens during the actual game or—to extend the metaphor—during the game of life? How important was that selection approach—put strengths in play, then manage weaknesses—to the overall success of the game? Do sports teams, or businesses, or universities that pick up the best talent usually enjoy the greatest successes? Intuition, anecdotal evidence, and—as we will see later—research results all seem to point to the answer being "yes!" As common sense as the strengths approach might sound, most of us tend to lose sight of it somewhere between primary school and adulthood (perhaps because of those unpleasant physical education experiences?). Somehow that initial strengths focus seems to fall away as we turn to fixing problems.

At work, many managers spend the lion's share of their time trying to shore up team weaknesses or correcting the deficit behaviour of a single "problem employee." In schools, teachers tend to notice the class clown or spend a disproportionate time managing the behaviour of the few rowdy kids. Yes, we have a knack for catching problems. Even in our private lives, most of us are painfully aware of our failings and deficits or those of our spouses. For adults, the message is sometimes backward: we don't need to attend to our strengths because they are working out just fine; instead, we need to work on overcoming our problems (just remember my student at Portland State University who I mentioned above!).

Alex Linley, the Director of the Centre for Applied Positive Psychology, discusses this phenomenon as the "Curse of Mediocrity."[1] Alex says that most folks have a strong desire to perform beautifully in almost every area of life. Because this is such an unrealistic goal, we are often left painfully aware of our shortcomings, and spend enormous resources and effort trying to overcome these "weaknesses." There is, however, something a bit short-sighted in this view. When we give short shrift to our greatest attributes, we undercut our potential. A problem focus betrays the idea that it is highly valuable to develop everything that is going well. After all, we still take our cars in for routine maintenance even when they are performing well, we still go to the doctor for physical check-ups even when we aren't sick and have no broken bones, and many of us still show up at the gym to increase our fitness (as opposed to decreasing our un-fitness). In other words: things don't need to go wrong to merit our attention.

The topic of strengths is one of the places that the science of positive psychology has made the greatest contributions, and will be the most useful to you in your professional work and personal life. There is now a large research literature suggesting that identifying and harnessing our best qualities can produce better results than trying to shore up our weaknesses. This can seem like a counter-intuitive idea, and some folks are slow to accept it. In organisations, for instance, there are many managers who swear by the approach that says they must carefully supervise their worst workers. Although this makes logical sense, in practical terms it is an attitude that frequently leads managers to using up the bulk of their time on a few poor producers while their real talent pool goes un-coached, un-directed, and un-managed.

Research from the Gallup Organization shows that paying attention to top performers and personal strengths can give individuals, teams, and organisations a cutting edge. You may remember that studies of the best managers showed that they emphasised strengths over seniority in making personnel decisions, had a tendency to match talents with tasks, and spent more time with their top producers. Similarly, studies of thousands of employees from dozens of industries show that workers who "have the opportunity to do what they do best every day" show less turnover, better customer loyalty, and higher productivity.[2] The chance to be at our best leads to feelings of effectiveness, worth, meaning and productivity. In short, workers (and students and clients) who have the opportunity to use their strengths feel more engaged. In fact, Alex Linley believes that this types of engagement is inherent in the definition of strengths themselves. He feels that one of the most important defining features of a strength is that it "energizes" a person.[3] Hopefully this resonates with you. You probably have had the experience of being "jazzed" or feeling excited when you were employing some of your top strengths.

It is important to raise a concern about weaknesses here. Some people feel uncomfortable with the idea that a person would focus wholly on strengths and ignore their weaknesses…. And with good reason. I do not advocate an approach to life that encourages folks to ignore their deficits and failings. Indeed, I think it can be important to be familiar with your weakest traits, and sometimes to try to overcome or compensate for them. That said, positive psychology research suggests there is tremendous mileage to be gained from attending to, developing, and employing strengths. People too easily fall into the trap of devoting enormous resources to overcoming natural weaknesses, despite the fact that these resources might be better suited to honing strengths. Alex Linley advises people to concentrate on growing their strengths but also acknowledges that, at times, there are very good reasons to attend to weaknesses. Thus, I do not advocate a Pollyanna approach that says you should always be at your best, or that you should always be happy, or that you should only concentrate on those activities at which you are best. In the end, former Gallup CEO Don Clifton echoes this sentiment when he counsels people that it is prudent to *manage* weaknesses so that they do not interfere with achievement, but *grow* strengths for the best shot at success.

Chris Peterson, a positive psychologist from the University of Michigan, uses the Gallup research and studies in positive psychology to make an important distinction: he distinguishes (as do the folks at Gallup) between engaged and unengaged workers.[4] Unengaged workers, according to Gallup, cost corporations enormous sums of money by turning away customers, making more health related claims, and having high rates of employee turnover.[5] This phenomenon, according to Peterson, represents the "disengaged worker fact." By contrast, there is—according to Peterson—a "happy worker hypothesis," in which engaged workers perform better. Although, undoubtedly, the difference between the top and bottom work groups can be chalked up to talent, it is also probable that praise, encouragement, and opportunities to exercise strengths play into the equation.

What are Strengths and How do We Recognise Them?

There are many historical antecedents to the science of strengths. Aristotle and other classical Greek thinkers catalogued a number of important personal virtues. Religions have similarly endorsed certain qualities such as sacrifice, hard work, and perseverance. In more recent times there has been some attention to the potential benefits of a strengths focus in the fields of social work, business management, and education. The psychological study of strengths began, perhaps, in the 1930s with Harvard researcher Gordon Allport.[6] Allport was interested in defining and studying key traits such as friendliness and enthusiasm, those that we typically think of as "personality." He believed that people have certain defining and unique characteristics, which are largely inborn. These overarching personality leanings, according to Allport, are—in part— what guides decisions and behaviour. Allport's intellectual legacy likely colours the way you think about people….. you probably think of the folks you know as having relatively immutable characteristics such as being an extrovert, having a quick temper, or being generous. You probably think of these traits as being fairly consistent from time to time, such that a person who is considerate and thoughtful today when her in-laws visit will likely also be considerate and thoughtful next year when she takes a new job. In his pioneering of personality theory, Allport advocated for a strong empirical foundation for research on traits to help differentiate this course of study from philosophy, religion, and morality. Unfortunately, Allport's study of character traits and virtues was supplanted by the more pressing concerns of mental illness exhibited by veterans of World War II. Only more recently have psychologists turned their attention to the classification and understanding of strengths.

One of these was Raymond Cattell, a British psychologist who spent the middle of the last century conducting research on personality at the University of Illinois.[7] Cattell catapulted the study of personality and—tangentially—strengths forward. He took the somewhat unwieldy list of 4,000 traits that Allport had identified and reduced them, statistically, to 16 common factors. These included 8 bi-polar categories such as "Outgoing-Reserved," "Upbeat-Sombre," and "Conscientious-Impulsive." Now, there are some fair criticisms of Cattell's schema…. Perhaps you don't think "humble" is the counterpoint to "assertive" or that "timid" should be paired with "adventurous." But, despite any statistical virtues or intellectual drawbacks, Cattell's model is noteworthy in that it allows for strengths and begins to create a formal taxonomy of people's best qualities. His model suggests that people — all people — are going to have a strength somewhere. For one person it might be conscientiousness, and for another it might be emotional stability. Cattell's work was important because it represented a new, scientifically sophisticated way of categorizing people's qualities, and allowed for strengths as well as weaknesses.

In the 1970s and 80s, psychologist Don Clifton, then head of the Gallup Organization, became interested in strengths. Clifton was a true positive psychology pioneer in that he was among the first modern psychologists to ask "what is going right with people?" From his vantage point at the helm of a large international business, Clifton saw the tremendous potential of learning from people who are at their best. He suspected that there was much to be learned from top performers in the workplace, and set about collecting data from the best managers. Clifton and his colleagues came to believe that everyone has innate talents. Talents are authentic, empowering, and people are often passionate about them. The Gallup research on the talents of top performers led directly to the first widely used classification of strengths, the Clifton StrengthsFinder™.[8] The StrengthsFinder™ is a proprietary instrument Gallup uses to identify talents in workers. These include abilities such as "Winning Others Over," "Achiever," and "Empathy." If you have ever taken this assessment (you can receive a one time use passcode to take it on-line whenever you purchase certain Gallup books such as

Now, Discover your strengths or *StrengthsQuest*) you have firsthand experience with how rewarding it can feel to receive positive feedback about your best qualities. Gallup clients use the StrengthsFinder™ in many of their hiring, team building, and other human resources practices. It is a good way of placing individuals and creating teams that will work optimally. Although the StrengthsFinder™ is widely used by organisations, it has several limitations where our interests are concerned. First, because it is a proprietary measure you must pay to use it, and do not have full access to all the data ever collected with it. It also means that we won't be discussing it at length this week. Further, while it is especially appropriate to achievement related life domains such as work and education the StrengthsFinder™ is not as applicable to relationships or other domains.

If you are still wonting for a concise definition of strengths Alex Linley provides a beautiful one:

> *A strength is a pre-existing capacity for a particular way of behaving,*
> *thinking, or feeling that is authentic and energizing to the user, and enables*
> *optimal functioning, development, and performance.* [9]

I have always found this particular way of looking at strengths helpful. First, I love that a strength is a "capacity." This means it is active potential, like a fire burning inside you just waiting for the proper moment to be used. The emphasis on "authentic" also hits the bull's-eye because it suggests a degree of self knowledge is in order. Lots of folks might want strengths in various categories, they might like to think of themselves as courageous, or generous, or nurturing. I would love to be a night owl instead of a morning person or love sunny beaches as much as I enjoy snowy mountains. The truth is, though, that by design or influence, I am best in the early morning and complain about the heat far more than I ever grumble about the cold. Those are my authentic traits. Similarly, recognising that you are or are not (as the case may be) forgiving or creative can save you from beating your head against the wall trying to attain virtues that do not come naturally to you. Finally, the crucial point: strengths energize people. Authentic strengths have a way of engaging and recharging people. There is a kind of excitement that occurs when you use your top strengths. Not that you don't need to take a break and "sharpen the saw" as Stephen Covey advises, but you generally get pretty good miles per gallon, metaphorically speaking, where strengths are concerned.

4.2 Reflection

Consider your own strengths. What are some of your shiniest qualities that come immediately to mind? What do other people say about you when they give you compliments? How were you praised growing up and at school? How much do you feel like you use these strengths? How much of your current success do you attribute to them? How much do you work on shoring up weaknesses? Feel free to write your answers here:

The VIA

It was Allport's work, as well as Clifton's, as well as that of others that influenced positive psychology researchers Chris Peterson and Martin Seligman as they approached the topic of strengths.[10] In early 2000, Seligman dreamed up the idea of creating a formal classification of strengths. Psychiatry and psychology have long had formal taxonomies of mental illness, in the form of the Diagnostic and Statistical manual of Mental Disorders, or DSM for short. The DSM is, essentially, a book of symptoms associated with various psychological maladies such as depression and anxiety that clinicians can use to diagnose and plan treatment for mental disorders. "Wouldn't it be nice," Seligman mused, "if we had a similar taxonomy by which we could diagnose strengths in people?" Admittedly, the idea has obvious curb appeal. Picture sending your children to a school where they were tested each year to see what they were great at. Imagine a university admission form that asked "When are you at your best" instead of the hackneyed "Please, briefly describe your strengths and weaknesses."

In fact, I am here reminded of a piece of lore from my own family: Many years ago my sister, Mary Beth, was applying to a number of graduate programmes in clinical psychology. One particular day she made the two hour drive to a school for an afternoon interview. However, en route she witnessed a terrible accident. A long-haul truck in front of her jack-knifed, flipped, and slid off the freeway. Mary Beth immediately pulled over and rushed to the truck. She climbed in through the broken windshield and began helping the injured driver. She asked his name, assessed his injuries to the best of her ability, and stayed with him to calm him until the paramedics arrived. As you might have guessed, she arrived at her interview late, dishevelled, and with a fair amount of dried blood on her dress. The admissions staff, as you can well imagine, were extremely impressed with her mettle. They did everything short of offering her entry on the spot (a couple of weeks later they formally accepted her). What is so interesting about this story isn't that it showcases my sister's bravery or quick-thinking, but rather, it suggests that these qualities can be used diagnostically to great advantage. The admission directors were not wrong either: Mary Beth went on to have stellar performance at school and a highly successful career after.

Armed with the idea that measuring strengths is possible and useful, Peterson and Seligman set about the monumental task of trying to identify personal strengths that would be relatively universal. They understood that certain virtues, such as punctuality, are culturally specific and would not be useful to everyone nor would they endure the test of time. In their search for ubiquitous strengths, Peterson and

Seligman turned to a vast body of religious and philosophical work. They read the Bible and the Koran and the Bhagavad-Gita. They read Aristotle and Kant and Augustine. They looked at classic works of literature, antiquated etiquette books, the Boy Scout Oath, and even the Klingon Code from the popular Star Trek television series. From these many sources they culled core virtues that appeared to have been advocated across time and across cultures. In the end, Peterson and Seligman developed a candidate list of 24 strengths of character that they believed to be universal. Indeed, I took this same list to research participants in Northern Greenland, rural Kenya, and the American Midwest to find out how they translated across cultures. It turns out that people from these diverse cultures recognised the 24 strengths, thought they were useful and desirable, thought they existed in men and women as well as in young and old people, believed there were cultural institutions in place that nurtured these strengths, and generally wanted their children to have these traits. The list of the 24 strengths is below:

The 24 Character Strengths identified by Peterson and Seligman (2004) and their Core Virtues. Adapted from Peterson & Seligman (2004, pp. 29-30).[11]

Wisdom and Knowledge: Those that entail the acquisition and use of knowledge

1. *Creativity:* Thinking of novel ways to do things
2. *Curiosity:* Taking an interest in ongoing experience
3. *Open-mindedness:* Thinking things through and examining counter-arguments
4. *Love of learning:* Mastering new skills, topics, and knowledge
5. *Perspective:* Providing wise counsel to others

Courage: Those that involve the exercise of will to accomplish goals in the face of opposition

6. *Bravery:* Not shrinking from threat, challenge, difficulty or pain
7. *Persistence:* Finishing what one begins
8. *Integrity:* Presenting oneself in a genuine way
9. *Vitality:* Approaching life with excitement and energy

Humanity: Those that involve tending and befriending others

10. *Love:* Valuing close relationships
11. *Kindness:* Doing favours and good deeds for others
12. *Social intelligence:* Being aware of the motives and feelings of others and of oneself

Justice: Those that underlie healthy community life

13. *Citizenship:* Working well as a member of a team or group
14. *Fairness:* Treating all people equally
15. *Leadership:* Encouraging a group to get things done

Temperance: Those that protect against excess

16. *Forgiveness and mercy:* Forgiving those who have done wrong
17. *Humility / Modesty:* Letting one's accomplishments speak for themselves without seeking the spotlight
18. *Prudence:* Being careful about one's choices
19. *Self-regulation:* Regulating what one feels and does

Transcendence: Those that forge connections to the larger universe and provide meaning

20. *Appreciation of beauty and excellence:* Noticing and appreciating beauty and excellence
21. *Gratitude:* Being aware of and thankful for good things happening
22. *Hope:* Expecting the best and working to achieve it
23. *Humour:* Liking to laugh and bringing smiles to other people
24. *Spirituality:* Having coherent beliefs about one's purpose and meaning

4.3 Reflection

Take a look at the list of 24 character strengths above. How accurate or complete do you think this list is? Did Peterson and Seligman include most of those traits you consider important? Are there virtues missing that you would add? Are there strengths on the list that you think do not belong there? Feel free to write your answers here:

Peterson and Seligman developed a measure of these strengths called the Values in Action (VIA) survey. The instrument is web-based, free of charge, and helps people to identify their top five signature strengths. The assessment can be accessed on-line at **www.viastrengths.org** (it requires a quick registration but is free and confidential). The VIA is a fairly long test, taking between 20 and 45 minutes depending on reading speed and the speed of the internet connection. The VIA is scored ipsatively, meaning that it presents the strengths in their rank order for each individual, and does not compare individuals against one another. Among the best features of the VIA is how well-researched and widely used it is. The VIA strengths have been compared across 54 nations,[12] across military and civilian samples,[13] linked to life satisfaction,[14] and shown to be a possible factor in recovery from illness,[15] and related to organisations.[16]

The VIA can be a helpful tool for you to use with your clients or students. In my own coaching practice I frequently have clients take the VIA so that we can later discuss how they might best employ their strengths to solve a problem or see an idea through. Most clients are attracted to the positive nature of the VIA and enjoy receiving positive feedback about what they do best. Interestingly, many people are surprised by some of their VIA results. It is not uncommon to hear statements such as "I knew I was a curious person, but I never thought of myself as brave!" This is especially true of the students in my positive psychology class at Portland State University. Strengths such as forgiveness, leadership, and creativity often take them unaware. Often, these types of surprising VIA results can lead to fruitful conversations that help clients and students appreciate strengths they have previously overlooked. Reminding the client that bravery includes speaking up to defend someone in a team meeting, for example, can help them accept and take ownership of the strength. Talking with them about the fact that creativity not be limited to the visual arts, it might mean spawning new ideas, making novels connections, using clever wordplay can really open their eyes to possibilities for using their strengths and pave the way toward accepting them.

Seligman, Peterson, and their colleagues conducted a controlled experiment in which they tested the effectiveness of a variety of positive psychology interventions such as expressing gratitude.[17] Among these interventions were two specifically related to the VIA: identifying one's strengths and intentionally using a strength during the week. Both interventions showed better than chance effectiveness, and—on average— led to decreased depression and increased happiness in the research participants. Here is another potential use of the VIA with clients, supervisees, and students. You can work with people to consciously identify and employ a particular strength, encouraging them to use the strength when addressing problems or making important decisions. In my experience, people really warm to this exercise and enjoy the opportunity to use their best qualities. Occasionally, however, people think they ought to be working on their weakest areas, and do not understand the rationale behind employing strengths. Sometimes these folks are swayed by research on positive psychology, other times they participate in the activity on a lark. In most cases, people who are motivated by this exercise and put in the effort report that it is enjoyable, engaging, and leads to feelings of happiness and purpose.

4.4 Reflection

Take a moment to consider which of the 24 VIA strengths really resonate with you. Do you have particular insight into some of them? Picture how you might work with a client around this particular strength. What questions would you ask? What personal stories might you share? What sources of inspiration might you use? What insights could you offer?

Now, think about those VIA strengths that seem distant to you. Perhaps they are strengths you do not particularly value or just seem downright foreign. How do you think this dynamic might affect you if your client was to present with this as her top strength? How might you overcome any difficulties understanding or cherishing this strength? Feel free to write your answers here:

Beyond the VIA

Many psychologists, coaches, and consultants who learn about the VIA are so taken with it—and understandably so—that they sometimes forget to continue innovating their practice. Although the VIA is a remarkable instrument, it is certainly not the last word in strengths assessment. The VIA focuses heavily on character strengths while ignoring skills, talents, and abilities. It also misses out on many important everyday interpersonal dynamics. Alex Linley has identified a number of other strengths that can be useful to consider. *Bounceback*, for example, describes those people who are uniquely gifted at using troubling experiences to catapult themselves forward in life. *Bounceback* is more than simple resilience, it is the ability to reach new heights. Take another example: *Esteem Builder*. You probably recognise that there are folks—maybe even you—who are expert at building up others. People who seem to appreciate all the fine points of others and are able to say just the right thing to make them feel great. To a certain extent you, yourself, can keep an eye out for common strengths that are not described elsewhere. I'll give you a quick example: I know a number of people who seem to procrastinate until nearly the last moment and then work quickly and end up with an excellent result. Interestingly, many of these folks beat themselves up for this strategy. I, however, think it is natural to certain types of people. I think there are those who can sit around Monday through Thursday morning playing solitaire on their computers (no, I'm not talking about me!) and then suddenly flurry into action and finish everything they need to by Friday, and do it very well. We could call these people "Incubators." In any case, it is easy to see that their efficient high quality work style is actually a tremendous gift.

Often, when working with others in a professional capacity, it can be prudent to take stock of more than just strengths. It makes sense to examine resources, talents, skills, and other qualities that might help folks move forward. Similarly, it can be productive to move beyond the top 5 signature strengths. Rather than simply asking "How might you use your natural curiosity in this situation?" there might be more mileage to be gained from asking how constellations of strengths work together, how team strengths compliment one another, what strengths are being overlooked, or when strengths ought *not* to be used. As you gain more facility with the VIA, and other strengths approaches, these types of more skilled uses will come to you and you will be able to make the instrument sing.

Review of Main Points From Week 4

- Studies show the greatest gains are made from cultivating and using strengths while managing weaknesses.

- Everyone has strengths, and identifying and using your strengths can lead to tangible benefits at home and at work.

- We now have sophisticated measures of strengths and these can be used effectively with students and clients.

- A strengths-focus does not mean that we should neglect our weaknesses entirely.

Reading for Week 4

Peterson, C. (2006). *A primer in positive psychology*. New York: Oxford University Press.

Please read Chapter 6.

Straight from the horse's mouth, Chris Peterson, pioneer of modern strengths research, discusses the VIA strengths assessment in depth. This chapter works as an adjunct to this week's material in that Chris spends time differentiating between talents and strengths. He also presents a broad explanation of many interesting empirical findings about the VIA strengths. In particular, I direct your attention to the fascinating figure on page 158 that shows certain strengths tend to cluster together. This figure can be quite useful in looking at constellations of strengths. Consider how you might use this figure with your clients or students.

Key References from Week 4

1. Linley, A. (2008). *Average to A+: Realising strengths in yourself and others*. Coventry, UK: CAPP Press.
2. Clifton, D. & Harter, J. K. (2003). Investing in strengths. In K. S., Cameron, J. E. Dutton, & R. E. Quinn, (Eds), *Positive organizational scholarship: Foundations of a new discipline* (pp. 111-121). San Francisco, CA: Berrett- Koehler Publishers.

3. Linley, A. (2008). *Average to A+: Realising strengths in yourself and others.* Coventry, UK: CAPP Press.

4. Peterson, C. (2006) *A primer in positive psychology.* New York: Oxford University Press.

5. Rath, T., & Clifton, D. (2004). *How full is your bucket? Positive strategies for work and life.* New York: Gallup Press.

6. Allport, G. W. (1966). Traits revisited. *American Psychologist, 21,* 1-10.

7. Cattell, R. B. (1945). The principal trait clusters for describing personality. *Psychological Bulletin, 42,* 129-161.

8. Rath, T. (2007). *Strengths Finder 2.0.* New York, NY, US: Gallup Press.

9. Linley, A. (2008). *Average to A+: Realising strengths in yourself and others.* Coventry, UK: CAPP Press.

10. Peterson, C., & Seligman, M. E. P. (2004). *Character strengths and virtues: A handbook and classification.* New York: Oxford University Press.

11. Same as #10.

12. Park, N., Peterson, C., & Seligman, M.E. P. (2006). Character strengths in fifty-four nations and the fifty US states. *Journal of Positive Psychology, 1,* 118-129.

13. Matthews, M. D., Eid, J., Kelly, D., Bailey, J.K.S., & Peterson, C. (2006). Character strengths and virtues of developing military leaders: An international comparison.*Military Psychology, 18,* 57-68.

14. Peterson, C., Ruch, W., Beermann, U., Park, N., & Seligman, M. E. P. (2007). Strengths of character, orientations to happiness, and life satisfaction. *Journal of Positive Psychology, 2,* 149-156.

15. Peterson, C., Park, N., & Seligman, M. E. P. (2006). Greater strengths of character and recovery from illness. *Journal of Positive Psychology, 1,* 17-26.

16. Peterson, C. & Park. N. (2006). Character strengths in organizations. *Journal of Organizational Behaviour, 27,* 1149-1154.

17. Seligman, M. E. P., Steen, T., Park, N., & Peterson, C. (2005). Positive psychology progress: Empirical validation of interventions. *American Psychologist, 60,* 410-421.

Further Reading

Buckingham, M., & Clifton, D. O. (2001). *Now, discover your strengths.* New York: Simon & Schuster.

Linley, A. (2008). *Average to A+: Realising strengths in yourself and others.* Coventry, UK: CAPP Press.

Peterson, C., & Seligman, M. E. P. (2004). *Character strengths and virtues: A handbook and classification.* New York: Oxford University Press.

4.5 Further Reflections

You may already have an intuitive sense that working with strengths is fun and beneficial. Indeed, you might already use this approach with students, supervisees, or clients. Regardless of your experience with this approach, it can be helpful to spend time thinking about strengths so you are more conversant with them as a concept.

Do you believe there is an optimal use of strengths? That is, at some point do you believe that strengths can be overused or destructive? Can strengths become weaknesses? If so, how, when, and why might his happen? Are there certain situations that call for a particular strength, or might most strengths be applied to almost any circumstance?

4.6 Exercises

It is difficult to work with client or student strengths unless you first have some experience with the relevant assessments and interventions. Use this week to familiarize yourself with the VIA and strengths interventions so that you can use them effectively in your professional work.

1. Go to **www.viastrengths.org** and take the VIA assessment of strengths. What do you think of the instrument? How easy was it to take it? What will your clients think of it? What do you think of your top 5 signature strengths? Are there any that are surprising? Why? Consider asking someone else if they see evidence of the surprising trait in you.

2. Choose one of your top strengths, from the VIA, the Strengths Finder, or elsewhere, and work on intentionally employing it throughout the week. Consciously make an effort to approach your daily activities through the thematic lens of this strength. Actively employ the strength when you are faced with difficulties, stressful situations, or tough decisions. How does it feel to use this quality? What is the effect of using it even more than you normally might?

3. Practice attending to strengths in another person. Listen as your spouse, best friend, or colleague speaks to you and try to pick up on the strengths they have. What do they seem passionate about? What are their underlying values? When do you hear their voice rise or speed up? What seems to activate and empower them?

4. Try keeping an eye out for uncharted strengths over the rest of the week. Pay attention to the way your friends and colleagues use their time, what they do when they are along, how they interact with one another. See if you can identify a potential strength.

Week Five: A Case for Hope and Optimism

One of the most fantastic things about being human—as opposed to being a kangaroo or jackrabbit—is our unique ability to plan for the future. Because of the evolutionary gift of highly developed frontal lobes in our forebrains, we humans are able to think abstractly, plan, organise, and make decisions about the future in ways no other animal can. Sure, squirrels can hoard acorns for the winter and bears can find a place to hibernate, but these are instinctual, not a matter of deliberate choice or careful planning. You rarely hear about a squirrel who opted not to stockpile food, or one who chose to save up extra rations for two or three winters, "just in case." But these long-sighted volitional actions are precisely the type of things humans are uniquely qualified for. That is, we are more future-oriented than any other species. Consider....We can set goals, marshal our resources in the service of making gains, and even hope for a better day down the road. In fact, we can even sacrifice short term goals—including those that are quite attractive—in favour of making long-term gains down the road. Among the gifts of our future orientedness are hope and optimism.

As grand as being future-minded seems, it is also worth mentioning that there is a dark side to our ability to think about times to come. The idea of an uncertain future can be frightening and most folks can envision future failure and hardship just as easily as they can picture success. The ability to see potential negative consequences down the road can paralyze people in their decision making, and future-mindedness can become a curse. In fact, for many of your clients, it is precisely their vivid imaginings of an unsuccessful future that will prevent them from making the progress they want. As coaches, consultants, therapists, managers, and teachers, it is our job to help others use the best aspects of positive psychology - hope and optimism - to think productively about the future rather than be sucked into the vacuum of anxiety and fear. The science of positive psychology has produced some effective theories and interventions for facilitating a hopeful attitude. This week we will cover this research as well as discuss ways to help clients and students harness optimism to their own benefit.

One example of a fascinating line of research related to future-mindedness is studies of "affective forecasting," pioneered by Harvard psychologists Dan Gilbert and Tim Wilson. Affective forecasting refers to our ability to predict how we will feel at some point in the future. We make these kinds of predictions all the time: How happy might I be if I take the new job offer? How will I feel if I marry this woman? How might I feel if I move to the house in the suburbs? Will I be happier if I go to Oxford or to Cambridge, Harvard or Yale? These are not just rhetorical questions; we actually make an attempt at predicting what life will be like in the future and how we will feel about it. These common predictions of future happiness (or sadness, anger, etc.) are particularly important because they heavily influence our decisions. You are far more likely to get married if you envision a happy, rather than sad, life after the nuptials. Interestingly, Gilbert, Wilson, and their colleagues have found that people consistently mis-predict their future feelings.

Here are a few quick examples: Gilbert asked college students how they would feel if their school lost an important upcoming football game and asked young professors how they might feel if they were granted or denied tenure.[1] As you might imagine, the students predicted being very upset, as did the faculty members when they thought about being turned down for tenure. On the other hand, the young professors thought they would be elated if they were granted tenure. Gilbert followed up with these folks to see how they *actually* felt, and how this correlated with their predictions. He found that people generally predict in the correct direction—that is, they get it right that winning a game will feel good while losing will be disappointing. Where they routinely make errors, according to Gilbert, is in the intensity and duration of the feeling. People generally think that negative life events will profoundly affect them and that this emotional aftermath will drag on and on. The data suggest otherwise: while people take an emotional hit after a loss, it is usually less intense than they predicted and lasts a shorter period of time than they would have guessed. Thus, learning about the scientific results (some of them counter-intuitive) from studies of future-mindedness, hope, and optimism can be useful because these topics bear directly on your clients'/students' motivation, decisions, and behaviour.

5.1 Activity

Take a moment and consider the concept of "anticipation." What is it you are either looking forward to or dreading right now? Perhaps it is a dinner party this weekend; maybe it is completing a report at work; possibly it is a trip to the dentist. Whatever the case, try to determine what it is about the future event that leads to your positive or negative anticipation. Is it the likely pleasantness or unpleasantness of the event? With Gilbert's research in mind, how accurate do you think your predictions are? Can you think of similar instances in the past and compare your current future prediction to those? Feel free to write down any insights or answers here:

As professionals, words like "hope" and "optimism" can seem breezy and out of place in the work setting. Many executives and managers might raise their eyebrows if they were to find these topics in their metaphorical professional "in-boxes." Even so, it is worth our while to learn about hope and optimism. Hope, it turns out, is associated with a variety of desirable outcomes at work and in relationships. Simply put, an optimistic outlook can lead to a greater likelihood of success. Studies show that people who are hopeful about the success of future outcomes are more likely to work hard toward them and to persevere even when tasks are difficult.[2] Interestingly, optimism is also associated with people giving up on impossible tasks when alternatives are present, arguably a measure of time use efficiency.[3] Because our most treasured goals are inevitably met by life's natural hurdles and set-backs, hope interventions are a perfect ace-in-the-hole for professionals. It is hope that sees us through in dark times and helps us make progress toward those goals we most highly prize.

Obstacles to Hope and Optimism

Before we discuss the nuts and bolts of how to encourage hope in the people you work with, it makes sense to step back and ask important questions about the factors that interfere with hope. Everyone has had the experience of being hopeless. Perhaps it is in the final minutes of a game you are badly losing. Maybe it is the sense of being crushed under the weight of an enormous responsibility. Regardless of the specific instance, hopelessness is just the psychological equivalent of the phrase "I can't do it." In fact, this is exactly what many hopeless people tell themselves. Following this logic, it may be fruitful to consider why people feel they "can't do it."

There are, as it turns out, many common and predictable explanations. First, people sometimes feel they do not have adequate resources to reach the outcome they desire. We can call this *resource-focused hopelessness*. This could mean that they do not have the knowledge, the talent, the support, or the time they need to see a project through. Consider the complaints you have surely heard from friends or clients who are assigned projects at work and are given a small staff, inadequate budget, or too little time. They feel stressed out, they complain, and they do not like their work…. Even if they ultimately complete the assignment!

In other cases, people lose self-confidence because they see the goal as too overwhelming, even if they do feel they have adequate resources. We can call this *goal-focused hopelessness*. I had a client one time, for example, who took on the side project of writing a book. She received a decent sized advance and was a capable wordsmith but still felt petrified when she thought about starting the work. "It is so big!" she complained. "I can't imagine how I'll ever start it let alone finish it!" By viewing the task in its entirety, she felt overwhelmed by it. Ultimately, we discussed the project in terms of writing a section, a chapter, a page, and these smaller units of measurement allowed her to move forward. Identifying your clients' (or students') reasons for hopelessness can be helpful in knowing the proper course of action to increase optimism and motivation.

5.2 Reflection

Consider the source of hopelessness of someone you are working with, or have worked with. If it was rooted in a perception of inadequate resources, what might you do (or did you do) to address this? How might exploring ways to increase resources help? How might exploring ways to use other resources to compensate for the inadequate resources help? Is there an advantage to one of these approaches over the other?

If the source of hopelessness is grounded in feeling overwhelmed, how can you work with the person to strengthen her sense of capability? Boost confidence? Break the task into smaller bits? Reframe the task? Point out overlooked resources? Is there an advantage to any of these particular tactics? Feel free to write your answers here:

Another interesting issue related to hope for the future is that of realism. Some folks believe in an idea of "naïve optimism." That is, there is a commonly held view that hopeful people are often unrealistic while more cynical people are somehow more attuned to reality. Is this true? Aren't there times in which hope can be unrealistic? Aren't there people who set goals too high, where success is unlikely? Research on goals suggests that goals and resources have to be well-matched.[4] In fact, working on a good fit between goals and resources is at the heart of what we just discussed above related to *goal-* and *resource- focused helplessness*. But unrealistic optimism is not just a matter of goals. In the late 1970s researchers Margaret Matlin and David Stang published results suggesting that people who had a propensity to attend to positives and be happy also had a tendency to overlook negatives.[5] Matlin and Stang dubbed this phenomenon the "Pollyanna principle." Matlin and Stang's research provided some initial proof that dispositionally positive and hopeful folks might not be entirely realistic (but, it must be noted, this does not mean that are wildly unrealistic either). The critical question is this: is it problematic to be a Pollyanna? The popular belief is that it is, indeed, problematic. Pollyannas are thought to miss important problems. Pollyannas may stay in bad relationships longer, have unrealistic self-appraisals at work, or set themselves up for disappointments. In some sense, it is this very notion that has given hope, optimism, and happiness a bad reputation. The truth is—while extreme Pollyanna-ism might be problematic—happiness is directly linked to more productivity, more creativity, and more energy.[6] In general, happier people are better for business. (One exception to this is work that requires a high degree of detail-orientedness and some consideration of downside risk such as air traffic control work and legal work).

Finally, a note on the common fear of failure is warranted. Some people are understandably concerned that an emphasis on optimism could be oppressive. This notion is along the lines of the criticisms one often hears about happiness and too heavy an emphasis placed on positivity. Isn't it natural that some clients are afraid of failure? Shouldn't there be room for this natural fear? The answer to these questions is an unequivocal "yes!" Failure is a fact of life and the prospect of it naturally scares most folks. When there is a very high likelihood of failure, then it may be prudent to adjust hope to bring it in line with reality, or adjust the goal accordingly. On the other hand, meaningful goals often require risks—emotional, social, personal, and financial—and research shows that people are very sensitive to losses of this nature.[7]

An example: Imagine rolling a die and if it came up 1 through 3 you would win £100, but if it came up 4 through 6 you would lose £80. The chances of winning or losing are the same, but the potential win is greater than the prospective loss. Would you be willing to roll? For most folks, the prospect of losing that £80 "weighs" more heavily on people's minds than winning the larger sum, even thought the chances of either outcome are equal. The same holds true with life's larger gambles, whether they are new relationships, starting a home business, launching a new product, or trying to lose weight. As much as people want to succeed they can't help but be conscious of the downside risk. None of us wants to waste time, energy, money, or social connections on projects that fail.

As professionals then, it can be helpful to bear in mind that "getting cold feet" is a natural phenomenon, and one which ought to be met with sympathy and acknowledgment. It is also important to remember that failure isn't all bad; it is essential to growth. Inventor Thomas Edison is famous for having quipped, "I failed my way to success." On roughly his 10,000[th] attempt, when Edison finally made his electric light bulb work, he is reported to have said triumphantly that he "found 9,999 ways *not* to do it!"

Hope Theory

It is a hopeful attitude that is going to help motivate your clients and students, and keep their momentum up during the tough patches. No one wants to begin a project if they think it is doomed to failure and few people like to start on goals if they think success is completely out of their hands and is only a matter of luck. The late, great psychologist Rick Snyder spent most of his professional career developing and working with something called "Hope Theory."[8] According to Snyder, people have hope when three conditions are present: goals thinking (working toward a goal), pathways thinking (described below), and agency thinking (self-confidence). As professionals, this simple piece of information can be invaluable in working with clients to develop one or all of these areas to foster a can-do attitude.

Goals Thinking: Goals, it turns out, are fundamentally important to human psychology. Goals help structure our time, aid us in making tough decisions, give us a bulls-eye to shoot for, act as a yardstick by which we can measure personal progress, and offer us a tangible outlet for living our values. But not all goals are created equally. You may be familiar with the SMART acronym, which suggests that "good" goals share a particular architecture (they are specific, measurable, attainable, realistic, and time-lined). Many coaches, teachers, and trainers are familiar with the idea that for goals to function effectively, they must be relevant to the individual. Research from positive psychologists also shows that goals that are related to the theme of power are toxic to personal satisfaction while those related to affiliation, generativity, and spirituality appear to promote well-being.[9] It can be helpful to bear in mind the realism, theme, values congruency, and other features of goals when working with people to increase their optimism. Listen to the language your students or clients use when they discuss their goals. Pay attention to their level of emotional intensity: do they sound upbeat and energetic, or downtrodden and deflated? Attend carefully to the theme of the goal, to how realistic the goal sounds, and how well the goal matches the individual's resources. Each of these aspects offers a potential avenue for questioning and encouragement that can increase hope.

Pathways Thinking: Pathways thinking is a fanciful term that simply means, in lay speak, something like "creative problem solving." Optimistic people, according to Snyder and his colleagues, are those that can see many routes to achieving a goal. When obstacles arise, as they surely do, optimists are able to find new solutions and continue making progress. In the early history of railroads, designers in places like Switzerland and the American West were faced with the problem of mountains. The slopes of mountains are generally too steep to build tracks on, and yet, trains need to travel across rough terrain. We know today that some of those civil engineers must have been optimists because they found an impressive array of ways to get trains through the mountains. Some railroads use specially fitted "cog trains," that have a mechanism that prevents them from slipping down a steep incline. Others snaked around the mountains. Sill others used dynamite to blast through rocky obstacles. In each case, these designers were able to think around the problem and persevere even when obstacles presented themselves.

Work and life are no different for the people you work with than it was for railroad pioneers. Whether your client's goal is to "be a good stay-at-home mother," "make three new sales this month," "feel less depressed," or "launch a home business by the end of summer," there will be difficult problems and discouraging times. What separates optimists from pessimists is not how tough life can be—for life throws curve balls at everyone—but rather, how an individual copes with problems and moves forward. As a manager, therapist, coach, or teacher, you have a special opportunity to help facilitate pathways thinking in those you work with. This can be done in a variety of ways. First, the open ended powerful questions that are the mainstay of all good coaching can be used by professionals of all stripes to encourage creative thinking. In the face of a set-back, asking your clients or students questions like "What else might you do here?" "What have other people done to overcome a similar situation?" and "Name three different things you might do to address this problem?" These queries can spark new lines of solution-focused thinking.

Another tool common to coaching and team meetings—brainstorming—can also be effectively used by managers, teachers, and consultants. Pathways thinking can be facilitated by bouncing suggestions for solutions between a group of people. Brainstorming ideas is fun and creative, and coaches can facilitate this process by joining in with suggestions, and even making things silly to promote out-of-the-box thinking. Consider the example of a client I once worked with who wanted to start a natural home cosmetics business. She had developed great products, good market contacts, and even a catchy web site. Unfortunately, her original funding source dried up and she feared she would have to shut her business down before she even really got up and running. She came to coaching highly focused on the funding issue and seemed to dwell on the single source of funding. I began by trying a solutions-focused orientation, asking how she had come about her original funding, and pointing out that she had past success in fundraising. Then, I offered to brainstorm new funding ideas with her. To lighten the mood and set the tone for some playful ideas I asked if I could tell her a quick joke. I keep a store of non-offensive silly, sometimes stupid jokes, for just such occasions. We then set up the structure for the brainstorming in which we would take turns throwing out ideas, one after another without taking the time to think about whether they were good or not. I started with the obvious: take a loan from the bank. She countered with: have a fundraising party. I wanted her to get creative, really creative, so I suggested: write Oprah Winfrey, Bill Gates, and five other billionaires asking their foundations for money. She said: Borrow from friends and family. I was still eager to see her expand her thinking so I countered by saying: unfurl a banner on the Eiffel tower with the web address where people could make donations! She began to catch on, coming back with: I could steal the money!

Around and around we went, our ideas ranging from the mundane (I could save up for it) to the fantastic (I could just run my business at a loss without care for money). By working together we were able to generate a list which was more creative and more thorough than anything we could have arrived at individually. After our brainstorming, we were able to sift back through the ideas and pull out those that had merit; those that fit with my client's values and aligned with her personal resources. In the space of only ten minutes my client changed from a problem-focused pessimist to an optimistic woman who had several workable funding ideas that she was eager to pursue ranging from loans to fundraisers to strategic partnerships.

5.3 Activity

Consider one minor problem you are currently facing. For the purposes of this exercise it should be only a small hurdle rather than a major obstacle. Perhaps you are irritated by road construction that is making your commute longer than usual. Maybe you have a tight deadline. Perhaps you are anxious about missing your child's school play because of work obligations. Here is a great chance to practice pathways thinking by brainstorming. Write down 20 possible solutions to your problem! Feel free to be absurd, grandiose, and creative. If you want to include "build a robot to do my work for me" then go ahead. You may want to consider watching a funny movie or reading a humorous comic before you begin to put yourself in a good mood. Don't get hung up on realism, or worry too much about spelling and grammar. Just go for it. When you are finished, notice how you feel. Consider your attitude toward the problem. Examine your list to see which solution or solutions have the greatest potential to work. Feel free to write your list here:

As a professional working with others, it may be helpful to bear in mind—where pathways thinking is concerned—that your own vitality can affect the hope of those you work with. One of the catalysts of major attitude change can be the fact that you, yourself, are not personally hassled by the hardships and setbacks of your clients. Your can-do attitude can be infectious, and even suggesting a brainstorming session carries with it the implicit idea that a solution is possible. While not every solution works out, or every session produces a perfect solution, professionals and clients alike can take heart in the knowledge that, no matter what, there is always another way to think about things.

Agency Thinking: The last crucial aspect of Hope Theory, according to Snyder, is self-confidence, which he calls "agency thinking." Agency thinking means a person believes he or she is capable of achieving an objective. This makes sense: people will be more optimistic about achieving their goals if they are confident in their own abilities to do so. Folks with low self-esteem, or those who doubt their abilities are far less likely to work hard, persevere in the face of hardship, or take risks that might lead to success. If self-confidence is a key feature of optimistic people then you are in luck. Boosting confidence is relatively easy to do.

There are two remarkably simple, yet powerful methods for boosting self-confidence. First, by acknowledging the strengths and successes of the people we work with, we can stroke egos in a way that is authentic. When we praise our students or celebrate a win with our clients we are not flattering them or manipulating them, we are in earnest. The best acknowledgments, in my experience, are those that focus on core client strengths rather than in-the-moment achievements. While it certainly feels good to hear a colleague say, "I am really impressed, you delivered a great power point presentation even though you were nervous. Good job!" this emphasises only momentary success. Imagine instead, commenting on your friends and colleagues in a more central way, as in "I am really impressed with your courage. You were nervous about the presentation and went ahead with it anyway. This fits so well with my picture of you as a courageous person, which I admire!" Acknowledging core strengths and virtues, as opposed to 'a job well done,' tends to raise self-esteem and self-confidence which, in turn, can boost optimism.

The second confidence booster is a formal "solutions focus" approach. Solutions focus was a new approach to psychotherapy developed by Insoo Kim Berg and Steve de Shazer.[10] This husband and wife team suggested that we could look at past success, rather than past failures, to learn how to cope with current problems. There are a variety of techniques used in solutions focus work (whether therapy, coaching, or otherwise) including interviewing for exceptions (tell me about a time when you weren't experiencing this problem…. What was happening then?), scaling questions (if you are an X on a 1 to 10 scale, what is preventing you from slipping down one point?), and coping questions (what has allowed you to come as far as you have?). While the specific techniques of solutions focus require training and experience, the basic underlying principles do not: every client has experienced success and, as professionals, we can point to those past victories to boost our clients' sense of self-efficacy.

5.4 Reflection

Think about two personally relevant short terms goals. One should be a goal that you feel fairly optimistic about, and the other should be one—perhaps one you have already discarded- that you are less hopeful about. As you consider these two goals pay particular attention to your sense of personal control over them. How much do you feel like you have some control over the ultimate outcome of the two goals? Consider ways that you might gain more power over the outcome of these goals. How does this affect your hope for the goals? Feel free to write your answers here:

Despite the fact that acknowledgment and solutions focus are powerful and effective techniques, they do not always work. It is important to remember that even though you read about these interventions and have experienced some success with them, there are clients who will resist them. Positive psychology interventions are not one-size-fits-all, and there are clients who will want to focus on problems and be vigilant for their own failures. Don't beat yourself up if a particular technique doesn't work, or if a client baulks at a particular intervention. In fact, just at the point you begin to feel discouraged that your work isn't as effective as you hoped…. That is the time for pathways thinking. Try something new, get creative, work in alliance with your client and, together, you will find a way.

Perfectionism

A few words ought to be said about perfectionism. Modern life in western societies and inspiring stories of people who overcome tremendous odds to reach unimaginable heights have set the stage for a culture of perfectionism. Most folks think they ought to strive to be a "10 out of 10," and believe that high expectations are the only way to get the success they want. Olympic athletes, for example, thrill us with their pursuit of excellence and inspire us in their success. But people who strive to be 10s, and succeed, are few and far between. While striving for perfection at the Olympic level might make sense, it is probably less appropriate to your client who wants to open her own art studio or someone in sales who wants to be the top company performer every single month. For these types of highly driven people, being *excellent* is likely to be more rewarding, and more achievable, than being *perfect*. Remember the mantra: everyone wants to be successful, only perfectionists want to be perfect. Perfectionism, it must be noted, is toxic to optimism for most people. For the average client with a perfectionist attitude, you will likely find that they are all too often discouraged rather than highly motivated.

So, how do you work with a perfectionist? How does one balance the tension between the admirable goal of striving for extreme excellence and the very real danger of setting oneself up for failure? Nick Baylis, a positive psychologist in Cambridge, suggests that a person may be a perfectionist if he or she focuses too heavily on achieving a goal, and not enough on enjoying the process of achieving the goal.[11] Ultimately, life is about the work we do in service of goals rather than about the final success of goals. Whether it is at work or in our romantic relationships we tend to spend far more time and energy on progressing toward goals than we do in the moment we actually realise them. Steering clients' focus toward the journey, rather than the destination, may have unexpected consequences where optimism is concerned. By asking questions such as "What do you enjoy about the work you are currently doing?" and "Even if it took twice as long to reach your goal, why might you continue pursuing it?" can elicit important information that many clients overlook. There can be a tendency to forget to enjoy work and effort and failure and overcoming hardship, and to think only of that shiny moment when we reach the finish line. It may be helpful to remind some clients: without the race, there is no finish line. For many people, your clients included, this truth can be just the ticket to optimism. Instead of always striving for a 10, the knowledge that an 8 is still exceptional can lead folks to the insight that they have the power to see their projects to the finish line.

Review of Main Points from Week 5

- As breezy a topic as hope and optimism sound, they are entirely appropriate to the work and school setting. Studies show they are linked to desirable outcomes in these environments.

- Optimism does not necessarily mean being unrealistic.

- Goals and resources need to be matched well to one another.

- You can increase hope by increasing creativity or self-confidence.

- Failure and fear of failure are natural and worthwhile.

- Perfectionism is toxic to well-being.

Reading for Week 5

Peterson, C. (2006). *A primer in positive psychology*. New York: Oxford University Press.

Please read Chapter 5.

It is important for you to know that although we use the words interchangeably in English psychologists distinguish between "hope" and "optimism." I have chosen to emphasise hope theory because I think it is useful and easy for professionals and clients to understand. Rest assured, this week Peterson offers a fine introduction to the parallel concept of optimism. He discusses dispositional versus cultivated optimism, optimism as a way of thinking (an explanatory style), and a more in-depth look at pessimism.

Key References from Week 5

1. Gilbert, D. (2006). *Stumbling on happiness*. New York: Knopf.

2. Segerstrom, S., & Nes, L. (2006). When goals conflict but people prosper: The case of dispositional optimism. *Journal of Research in Personality, 40*, 675-693.

3. Aspinwall, L., & Richter, L. (1999). Optimism and self-mastery predict more rapid disengagement from unsolvable tasks in the presence of alternatives. *Motivation and Emotion, 23*, 221-245.

4. Diener, E., & Fujita, F. (1995). Resources, personal strivings, and subjective well-being: A nomothetic and idiographic approach. *Journal of Personality and Social Psychology, 68*, 926-935.

5. Matlin, M., & Gawron, V. (1979). Individual differences in Pollyannaism. *Journal of Personality Assessment, 43*, 411-412.

6. Lyubomirsky, S., King, L., & Diener, E. (2005). The benefits of frequent positive affect: Does happiness lead to success? *Psychological Bulletin, 131*, 803-855.

7. Novemsky, N., & Kahneman, D. (2005). The boundaries of loss aversion. *Journal of Marketing Research, 42*, 119-128.

8. Snyder, C. R. (1994). *The psychology of hope: You can get from there from here*. New York: Free Press.

9. Emmons, R. (1999). *The psychology of ultimate concerns: Motivation and spirituality in personality*. New York: Guilford Press.

10. Jackson, P Z. & McKergow, M. (2007). *The solutions-focus: Making coaching ad change simple* (2nd ed.). London: Nicholas Brealey.

11. Baylis, N. (2005). *Learning from wonderful lives: Lessons from the study of well-being brought to life by the personal stories of some much admired individuals.* Cambridge, UK: Cambridge Well-Being Books.

Further Reading

Seligman, M.E.P. (1991). *Learned optimism*. New York: Knopf.

Snyder, C.R. (1994). *The psychology of hope: You can get from there to here*. New York: Free press.

Special note: I spent the bulk of this week discussing Snyder's work, in large part because his theory is simple, attractive, and easy-to-use. Seligman has also written a very fine book and for those of you wanting to dig a little deeper or see the topic presented in a different way I recommend this book.

5.4 Reflections

You have experienced many times in your life when you have been optimistic. You have experienced the excitement and charge that hopeful anticipation can bring. Similarly, you have first-hand experience of feeling deflated, beaten, and pessimistic. Taking time to reflect on these experiences in your own life can help you better understand the concepts presented this week, and use them more effectively with the people you work with.

Think about an area of your life in which you feel confident and capable. Perhaps you are an excellent public speaker, a strong tennis player, or a good mother. Try to identify which skills, talents, passions, and strengths lead to your feelings of confidence. Next, consider how this confidence affects you: how do you think about problems, setbacks, and hardships related to this domain of life? How is this different than how you approach similar problems related to domains in which you are less confident?

5.5 Exercises

Although hope and optimism are a natural part of life they are concepts that often slip under our perceptual radar or are taken for granted. Try these activities to raise your awareness of hope and optimism in yourself and others.

At work, pay attention to the way your colleagues discuss future events, whether they are upcoming trade shows, team meetings, sales deadlines, or presentations. Pay particular attention to their posture, facial expressions, voice, language, and level of energy. Where would you place them on a continuum of optimism-pessimism? Do they dread the future event? Are they anxious about it? Do they seem disengaged or uninterested? Are they eager or enthusiastic? What clues tell you this is the case?

A Resource for Professionals: Hope Questions

1. How would you know if you were successful in this goal?
2. What would not attempting this goal cost you?
3. Which of your past goals have you succeeded in?
4. What led to that success?
5. Tell me about a time when you were not facing this problem.
6. How have you overcome similar problems in the past?
7. How have other people overcome similar problems in the past?
8. Tell me about the resources you have that might help with this problem.
9. How optimistic are you that you will reach this goal?
10. What leads you to be as optimistic as you are?
11. Regardless of success or failure, what do you enjoy about working on this project each day?
12. If this problem were happening to a friend, what might you tell her?
13. Tell me about a time that you could have given up but didn't.
14. Tell me three different ways you might overcome this hurdle.
15. If this problem were to suddenly disappear, what would your life be like? How would you know? How different is that situation than what your life is like now?
16. Tell me about a time when you were at your best. How might you use some of your best attributes in this situation?
17. Remind me of the success you have already experienced on this project.
18. If you could snap your fingers and magically find the strength to persevere, what would that look like? What would allow you to persevere now?
19. Here is what I have always admired about you: X, Y, Z.
20. Tell me which of your strengths and virtues your spouse or friends might brag about.

Week Six: Putting It All Together

I believe you should start this final week by patting yourself on the back. It has been six full weeks since you began this course and—hopefully—you have undergone a transformation. I hope sincerely that you began this intellectual journey as someone who was curious about positive psychology and its possible uses at work, but have evolved into someone who has a solid foundation of learning about the topic. Consider all we have covered together: you have acquired expertise in content areas as diverse as happiness and optimism. You have learned about the many merits of a strengths focus, and have been given the tools to apply these topics to your work. You have, ideally, had time to test the exciting idea that harnessing strengths, as opposed to shoring up weaknesses, is a valid route to success. Hopefully, by now you have had the opportunity to absorb this fascinating new information, practice fundamental positive psychology skills with friends, colleagues, or family members, and—perhaps—use interventions with actual clients. It would be greatly reassuring to me if you shared my same sense of having come a long way in a short time. You deserve a round of applause for your efforts.

In keeping with the general spirit of professional growth and development that is inherent to positive psychology, it is time to push yourself to new heights even as you savour the successes you currently have under your belt. It is time to integrate the skills and knowledge you have gained over the past weeks, and use them together in your professional work. When you are able to synthesize what you have learned in this course you will move from being a knowledgeable novice in positive psychology to someone who is gaining mastery. It is also here that I will confess that I am very proud of the fact that I do not believe that your learning stops simply because we have arrived at our final week together. It is an unfortunate fact that many positive psychology courses and programmes cover a broad spectrum of topics, but provide little information on continued professional development or on keeping up with new research. Because positive psychology is a science it is, by definition, a dynamic body of knowledge. New findings emerge with regularity. It is important—even vital—that you periodically update your knowledge of new developments in positive psychology and seek to improve your skills set. This week, you will be encouraged to stay at the cutting edge of positive psychology, and be given specific tools for doing so. The best news is, you are prepared for it! If you have been keeping up with the content of this course, and have been practicing with the suggested exercises, you are ready to take positive psychology to the next level.

As proof of how far you have come, go back and look at the questions you answered way back in Week 1. That week you were asked to list what attracted you to positive psychology, what scepticism you harboured toward the subject, and what you wanted to get out of this training. You are now in a perfect position to evaluate just how much you have learned. Has your scepticism been addressed? Have many of your curiosities and questions been answered? Have you achieved the goal you set for yourself? Take the time and carefully consider the answers to these questions. For those questions that remain unanswered, you even have some exciting avenues for further exploration.

Professional Development: Becoming a Great Positive Psychology Practitioner

Most professionals, whether they are coaches, or lawyers, or psychotherapists, believe in professional development. Simply put, professional development is a commitment to learning new skills and keeping expertise updated. Most professions even have requirements for continuing education to ensure competence and best practices. This is a sensible approach to career growth, and is likely to lead to responsible work. That said, it makes sense to wonder whether this approach to professional development is enough to challenge people to move from responsible practice to exceptional practice. Excellence in professional work comes from a combination of factors ranging from natural talent to professional experience to innovation. You are highly encouraged to look at professional development as more than simply adding occasional new tools to your working toolbox. Instead, consider the additional power of innovation and strategy for your practice.

When folks consider the activities of their work they tend to think of their job descriptions and assigned duties. Few people think of innovation. Innovation is often a word we associate with science, medicine, and technology. But innovation is a major part of raising the bar on professional work, which is very much in line with the philosophical side of positive psychology. The people who really set themselves apart in their use of positive psychology are folks who take existing assessments and interventions and are blending them or using them in novel ways. Take the example of the VIA strengths assessment. Most folks encourage the people they work with to take the VIA, identify their top five signature strengths, and then work with those. This all too common approach—while sensible and effective— does not reflect the most cutting edge practice of positive psychology. What if you focused on the next five strengths as being "potential" or "latent" strengths? What if you began paying attention to particular constellations of strengths, looking at how unique pairs work in concert with one another? What if you kept an eye out for strengths that are not represented on the VIA and considered ways to use them with your clients? I encourage you to take the initiative and use your creativity to apply positive psychology rather than waiting on experts to tell you what to do. Innovation has the additional benefit of keeping your work fresh and engaging for you.

Of course, innovation is easier said than done. If innovation was a simple matter we would all be making huge weekly gains in our professional lives. I recommend setting aside time, either every week or every other week specifically to innovate. This protected time may be as small as a half hour. You may choose to do it in the car on the way to work, or you might prefer setting up a weekly call with a couple of creative colleagues with whom you enjoy sharing ideas. I have used both tactics myself and found both to be effective. Typically, how I approach an innovation session is by taking stock of new ideas I may have heard about in other professions, have read about in popular books or professional journals, or ideas I have for growing my business (to new markets, new service delivery modes, and so forth). Spend your innovation time jotting notes, brainstorming, and letting yourself be creative without concern for realism. You can always go back and evaluate the merits of your ideas later.

6.1 Innovation

Consider each area of positive psychology we have covered. Perhaps choose to think about one content area a week for the next several weeks. Ask yourself how you might use what you have learned creatively with your clients. Perhaps you will find new ideas for packaging your services such as workshops, e-courses, or consultancy tools. Maybe you will arrive at ideas for novel ways to use research on positivity, or think of particularly useful applications for hope theory. Ultimately, the idea is to harness the excitement and dynamism of positive psychology to move your professional life forward. Write your answers here:

Another area to consider in your professional development is "strategy." Many professionals attend workshops and trainings aimed at teaching new skills. It is common to receive training in the latest tools or most popular new professional methods. Too often, however, these courses do not teach people how and when to optimally employ their new skills. They simply hand the tool and assume you will recognise where and when best to use it. Positive psychologist Barry Schwarz even raises this criticism about how people use their strengths. It is one thing, Schwarz argues, to possess and use personal virtues. It is quite another to know when to use them, how to best use them, and when to refrain from using them. It is one thing to be courageous, and quite another to know where your courage is best served and when other strengths are called for instead. The secret to success, according to Schwarz lies in "practical wisdom." Practical wisdom, according to Schwarz is a meta-skill by which we learn how to employ our gifts and talents optimally. Through accumulated experience you will learn which aspects of positive psychology work best, with which types of clients, and when it might be a good idea to talk about weaknesses instead of strengths. It may be helpful to remember the old adage, "If your only tool is a hammer, then everything looks like a nail." Positive psychology is a fantastic tool, but it is not the only tool. I would like to reiterate here that positive psychology can serve as a beautiful adjunct to the work you are already doing, and is not necessarily intended to replace it. Accumulated wisdom will help you use positive psychology strategically in your work so long as you take notice of what works and when.

Keeping up with Positive Psychology

Although positive psychology is a philosophy that says that people ought to capitalize on personal strengths and that happiness is highly beneficial, it is also a science. Because it is a science, positive psychology is a dynamic body of knowledge. Every month new research findings are published, theories are introduced, and applications are considered. One of the most important elements of using positive psychology on the job is staying abreast of the recent developments. Most people aren't sure where to look for new information and, even when they do find publications, most scientific articles are full of complicated statistical analyses. Keeping up with positive psychology, then, is a matter of knowing where to look for information that is appropriate to your work, and written in a language you can appreciate. Fortunately, there are many good sources for connecting with others who are interested in positive psychology and learning about the latest developments in the field:

Online Resources

There are a variety of web sites that offer digest versions of the latest studies as well as online forums for discussing positive psychology research and applications. You can also register for the free monthly Positive Psychology Bulletin from CAPP at **www.cappeu.org/bulletin.html** Other resources are also available:

1. *The Centre for Applied Positive Psychology* (CAPP). CAPP is an organisation dedicated to advancing and disseminating positive psychology research, and to developing and promoting its applications. This web site includes information on trainings, conferences, and user forums. **www.cappeu.org**

2. *The Positive Psychology Centre* (**http://www.ppc.sas.upenn.edu/**). This is Martin Seligman's home site and includes thorough information about the history, current events, and resources for positive psychology.

3. *VIA Strengths* (**http://www.viastrengths.org**). This is the official home page of the Values in Action Institute, the non-profit organisation that spearheaded the development of the VIA classification of strengths.

4. *Friends of Positive Psychology*. (Positive Psychology List Serve). This is the largest and most comprehensive online forum for positive psychology. It is free to join at: **http://lists.apa.org/cgi-bin/wa.exe?SUBED1=FRIENDS-OF-PP&A=1**

5. *Authentic Happiness*. Martin Seligman publicly launched positive psychology with the publication of his book, Authentic Happiness. Two Seligman-related sites have sprung up with a variety of news, forums, book recommendations, and other positive psychology information. **www.authentichappiness.com** and **www.reflectivehappiness.com**

6. *Positive Psychology News Daily*. This online newspaper is updated frequently by graduates of the prestigious Master in Applied Positive Psychology program at the University of Pennsylvania. The *Daily News* carries features and commentary on coaching, conferences, and book reviews. **www.pos-psych.com**

7. *The European Network for Positive Psychology*. This is the web site for the European network of professionals interested in positive psychology. It contains, among other things, a comprehensive list of meetings, trainings, and conferences on positive psychology held in the EU. **www.enpp.org**

8. *International Positive Psychology Association*. As of the time of this writing, the International Positive Psychology Association was being formed. It can be accessed online at: **www.ippanetwork.org**

9. *Researcher home pages*. You can often access PDF articles of the latest research and free assessment tools by visiting faculty web sites. Consider looking at those of Ed Diener, Sonja Lyubomirsky, Ken Sheldon, or any other researcher that you have come across who piques your interest.

Resources in Print

Publishing books on positive psychology has become something of a cottage industry in recent years. Each year sees the arrival of new titles, new points of view, and positive psychology applied in new ways. This list is limited to only a few exceptional sources:

1. *Average to A+*, by Alex Linley. This book is an intellectually rich look at strengths and their application in a wide range of life domains. Linley extends well beyond the VIA assessment of strengths to include a comprehensive look at the definition, measurement, and use of strengths.

2. *Authentic Happiness*, by Martin Seligman. This is the book that started it all. Seligman presents his view of a strengths focus and discusses both his personal journey to this philosophy and the exciting science that forms its foundation. He provides practice examples, tips, assessments, and applications for positive psychology.

3. *The Happiness Hypothesis*, by Jon Haidt. University of Virginia researcher Haidt discusses several important ideas that have withstood the test of time. He draws on sources as diverse as eastern philosophy, western religion, and modern science. His easy to read writing style makes the book perfect for those looking to expand their knowledge without getting a headache.

4. *Positive Psychology Coaching*, by Robert Biswas-Diener and Ben Dean. This is the seminal book in the field of positive psychology coaching. It is the first book to marry these two disciplines together and presents both a broad overview of positive psychology as well as many practical suggestions for applying it to coaching. This book includes chapters on "the future of positive psychology coaching" and three chapters on strengths coaching.

5. *How Full is Your Bucket?* By Tom Rath and Don Clifton. This slender volume by the former CEO of the Gallup Organization and his grandson is light but powerful. For anyone coaching people around work related issues this book is a must. In simple language Rath and Clifton spell out how positive psychology can be applied to jobs, and why.

In Person Resources

There are a variety of annual conferences, weekend trainings, tele-classes, and certificate programmes in positive psychology. These change frequently and can best be accessed through web searches or through the online sources listed above. CAPP provides an up-to-date newsletter and web site that contains links to many of these developments, the Positive Psychology Bulletin, as mentioned above.

Marketing Positive Psychology Responsibly

Although it may be a gross generalization, people fall into two broad camps when it comes to positive psychology. For the first group, positive psychology is a breath of fresh air. It provides a language, philosophy, and hard evidence for the type of upbeat, positive living that they value. For these folks positive psychology can seem like an epiphany. Whether this describes you or your clients this is a group who does not need to be "sold" positive psychology. That is, they will take little convincing that this is a worthwhile way to look at the world. The other group of people will be somewhat sceptical of positive psychology. These could be managers or coaching clients who are concerned with productivity and the bottom line, and will want proof that positive psychology bears directly on these. The best way to approach this group is to understand them as a market, and know the outcomes they value. Based on your familiarity with them you can tailor the language you use to connect positive psychology directly to their values. Instead of talking about "increasing happiness in the workplace" you can talk about "increasing employee engagement." "Turnover and sick leave" are directly tied to "employee well-being," and "hope" can be reframed as "task perseverance." It is not simply a matter of linguistic gymnastics, however; it is important to remember that the research is on your side. There is a compelling case to be made based on the research in positive psychology that, by any name, these tools are effective.

In the End

In the end it can be reassuring to know that you are not alone in your interest in positive psychology. Positive psychology is a refreshing orientation to life, and one that has steadily been increasing in popularity. More and more professionals are becoming aware of this promising discipline, and many have gone through positive psychology courses or purchased books on the topic. You are in a wonderful position in that you are getting in on the relative ground floor of positive psychology, but not so early as to have to fight to establish the legitimacy of the field. You can take heart in the knowledge that you have a community of bright and enthusiastic peers who are eager to share their learning and ideas with you over internet forums and at conferences. You are in a perfect position to learn about positive psychology, tailor it to your own needs, and apply it in dynamic new ways.

You have come a long way in the six weeks of this course. You have been introduced to new information and asked to apply it to real life situations. Hopefully, learning about positive psychology has influenced the way you think about people and the world. Ideally, you are more vigilant for strengths and success, and value happiness and optimism more than ever. Armed with powerful questions, a positive outlook, and scientifically tested interventions, you are ready to apply positive psychology to your work. It is an exciting moment, and we wish you all the best.

6.2 Looking Back

Please use this time to return to Week 1, and review the exercises and "Looking Forward" section you completed at that time. Evaluate your level of skill and knowledge now as compared to when you first began this course. Be realistic about what you have achieved and what you would still like to learn or accomplish. Please answer the following four questions as your final reflective exercise for the course:

This is what I have learned about positive psychology and its applications:

This is how, as a result, I have used positive psychology in my work:

These are the areas that I still need / want to learn more about:

This is what I am going to do to learn about them:

Final Course Assessment

Please consider a work issue from your own life. It does not matter if you are a therapist, teacher, coach, or other professional. Considering all we have covered in this course please describe how you would adapt the positive psychology theory, assessments, and interventions to your work issue. For example, if you are a coach, please describe how you might work with particular client X, including your rationale, any local modifications that might have to be made, and why you might intentionally avoid certain techniques or concepts. Please write up your thoughts in a 600 word essay. I am not looking for right or wrong answers but, rather, want you to use this as an opportunity to synthesise and apply your learning.

Made in the USA
San Bernardino, CA
09 September 2014